CW00969325

WJEC EDUQAS GCSE

English Literature
Skills for Literature
and the
Unseen Poetry

Paula Adair

Series Editors:
Jonathan Harrington
Paula Adair

DYNAMIC LEARNING

HODDER
EDUCATION
AN HACHETTE UK COMPANY

The publisher would like to thank the following for permission to reproduce copyright material:

Acknowledgements: pp.7–11: Simon Armitage: from 'Manhunt' from *The Not Dead* (Pomona Press, 2008); **pp.33–7: Imtiaz Dharker:** from 'Living Space' from *Leaving Fingerprints* (Bloodaxe, 2009), reproduced by permission of Bloodaxe Books on behalf of the author, www.bloodaxebooks.com; **pp.43–7: Rita Dove:** from 'Cozy Apologia' from *American Smooth: Poems* (W.W. Norton, 2006); **pp.48–53: Carol Ann Duffy:** from 'Valentine' from *New Selected Poems 1984–2004* (Picador, 2004); **pp.59–63: Seamus Heaney:** from 'Death of a Naturalist' from *Death of a Naturalist* (Faber & Faber, 2006); **pp.64–8: Ted Hughes:** from 'Hawk Roosting' from *Lupercal* (Faber & Faber, 1985); **pp.75–9: Philip Larkin:** from 'Afternoons' from *The Whitsun Weddings* (Faber & Faber, 2001); **pp.90–4: Owen Sheers:** from 'Mametz Wood' from *Skirrid Hill* (Seren, 2005); **p.122: Alan Bold:** 'Autumn' © Alan Bold to Alice Bold, reproduced by permission of Alice Bold; **p.127: Berlie Doherty:** 'Playgrounds' from *Walking on Air* (Kindle Direct Publishing, 2014), reproduced by permission of David Higham Associates; **pp.128–9: Mary Oliver:** 'The Summer Day' from *New and Selected Poems: v.1* (Beacon Press, 2004), reproduced by permission of the publisher; **p.133: Owen Sheers:** 'Winter Swans' from *Skirrid Hill* (Seren, 2005); **p.135: Matthew Sweeney:** 'Zero Hour' from *Sanctuary* (Jonathan Cape, 2004), reproduced by permission of The Random House Group Ltd.; **p.142: Gareth Owen:** 'Song of the City' from *Song of the City* (Armada, 1987); **Brian Patten:** 'The River's Song' from *Thawing Frozen Frogs* (Frances Lincoln Children's Books, 2012); **p.146: Jenny Sullivan:** 'Rejection' (Pont); **Elizabeth Jennings:** 'Years Ago' from *Extending the Territory* (Carcanet, 1985); **p.156: Rupert M. Loydell:** 'Tramp' from *Fill These Days* (Exeter: Stride, 1990), © Rupert Loydell, reproduced by permission of the author; **Zulfikar Ghose:** 'Decomposition' from *Jets from Orange* (Macmillan, 1967), © 1967 Zulfikar Ghose, reproduced by permission of Sheil Land Associates on behalf of Zulfikar Ghose; **p.160: Tony Curtis:** 'Strongman'; **Dr Maya Angelou:** 'On Aging' from *AND STILL I RISE* (Little, Brown Book Group, 1986), reproduced by permission of the publisher; **p.162: Andrei Voznesensky:** 'First Ice'; **Georgia Garrett:** 'Manwatching'; **pp.164–5: Ted Hughes:** 'Wind' from *The Hawk in the Rain* (Faber & Faber, 2015); **James Berry:** 'Hurricane' from *Hutchinson Treasury of Children's Poetry*, ed. Alison Sage (Hutchinson, 1998); **p.167: Steven Blyth:** '3am Feed' from *So* (Peterloo Poets, 2001), © Steven Blyth, reproduced by permission of the author; **Eavan Boland:** 'Night Feed' from *Night Feed* (Carcanet, 1994); **p.169: Rita Dove:** 'Dawn Revisited' from *On the Bus with Rosa Parks: Poems* (W.W. Norton, 2000); **Stewart Conn:** 'Carpe Diem' from *The Touch of Time: New and Selected Poems* (Bloodaxe, 2014), reproduced by permission of Bloodaxe Books on behalf of the author, www.bloodaxebooks.com.

All exam guideline material reproduced by permission of WJEC.

Every effort has been made to trace or contact all copyright holders, but if any have been inadvertently overlooked the Publishers will be pleased to make the necessary arrangements at the first opportunity.

Photo credits: p.7 © GARY DOAK/Alamy; **p.9** © Lynn Hilton/ANL/REX_Shutterstock; **p.12** public domain/http://commons.wikimedia.org/wiki/File:Elizabeth_Barrett_Browning,_Poetical_Works_Volume_I,_engraving.jpg; **p.14** © Beryl Peters Collection/Alamy; **p.17** public domain/http://commons.wikimedia.org/wiki/File:William_Blake_engraved_by_W._C._Edwards.jpg; **p.19** © aluxum – Fotolia; **p.20** © nickolae – Fotolia; **p.23** http://commons.wikimedia.org/wiki/File:Letters_from_America,_Brooke,_1916,_frontispiece.jpg; **p.25** Australian War Memorial /http://commons.wikimedia.org/wiki/File:Australian_infantry_small_box_respirators_Ypres_1917.jpg; **p.28** © istockphoto/Getty/Thinkstock; **p.29** © oneinchpunch – Fotolia; **p.33** © Simon Powell/courtesy of Bloodaxe Books; **p.34** saiko3p – Fotolia; **p.39** © The Granger Collection, NYC/TopFoto; **p.40** sanderstock – Fotolia; **p.43** © Barbara Zanon/Getty Images; **p.45** © engy1 – Fotolia.com; **p.48** © GARY DOAK/Alamy; **p.50** © Rainer Plendl – Fotolia; **p.54** © Photos.com/Getty/Thinkstock; **p.56** © Wellcome Library, London. Copyrighted work available under Creative Commons Attribution only licence CC BY 4.0 http://creativecommons.org/licenses/by/4.0/; **p.59** Geraint Lewis/REX_Shutterstock; **p.61** © Allan Grant/The LIFE Picture Collection/Getty Images; **p.64** © NILS JORGENSEN/REX_Shutterstock; **p.66** © juancarlos1969 – Fotolia; **p.69** © Wellcome Library, London. Copyrighted work available under Creative Commons Attribution only licence CC BY 4.0 http://creativecommons.org/licenses/by/4.0/; **p.70** © eyetronic –Fotolia; **p.75** © Daily Express/Hulton Archive/Getty Images; **p.76** © Jon Lyons/REX_Shutterstock; **p.80** © The Art Archive/Alamy; **p.82** © TopFoto; **p.85** © Georgios Kollidas – Fotolia; **p.89** © Gilles BASSIGNAC/Gamma-Rapho via Getty Images; **p.90** © REX_Shutterstock; **p.92** © Chronicle/Alamy; **p.95** © nickolae – Fotolia; **p.97** Stephen Dorey - Bygone Images/Alamy; **p.122** © Khvost – Fotolia; **p.127** © THOMAS SAMSON/AFP/Getty Images; **p.130** © leekris – Fotolia; **p.133** © aboutfoto – Fotolia; **p.135** chokchaipoo – Fotolia; **p.142** © boule1301 – Fotolia; **p.144** ©Stéphane Bidouze – Fotolia; **p.145** Martinan – Fotolia; **p.146** © Dangubic – Fotolia; **p.159 left** © istockphoto/Getty/Thinkstock; **right** poco_bw – Fotolia; **p.162** © Balazs Kovacs Images – Fotolia; **p.165** © A. Karnholz – Fotolia; **p.167** © Monkey Business – Fotolia; **p.169** © denis_333 – Fotolia

Although every effort has been made to ensure that website addresses are correct at time of going to press, Hodder Education cannot be held responsible for the content of any website mentioned. It is sometimes possible to find a relocated web page by typing in the address of the home page for a website in the URL window of your browser.

Orders: please contact Bookpoint Ltd, 130 Milton Park, Abingdon, Oxon OX14 4SB. Telephone: (44) 01235 827720. Fax: (44) 01235 400454. Lines are open 9.00–17.00, Monday to Saturday, with a 24-hour message answering service. Visit our website at www.hoddereducation.co.uk

© Paula Adair 2015

First published in 2015 by

Hodder Education

An Hachette UK Company,

Carmelite House

50 Victoria Embankment

London EC4Y 0DZ

Impression number	5	4	3	2	1
Year	2019	2018	2017	2016	2015

All rights reserved. Apart from any use permitted under UK copyright law, no part of this publication may be reproduced or transmitted in any form or by any means, electronic or mechanical, including photocopying and recording, or held within any information storage and retrieval system, without permission in writing from the publisher or under licence from the Copyright Licensing Agency Limited. Further details of such licences (for reprographic reproduction) may be obtained from the Copyright Licensing Agency Limited, Saffron House, 6–10 Kirby Street, London EC1N 8TS.

Cover photo (and repeated use throughout) by Ria Osborne

Illustrations by Integra Software Services Pvt. Ltd.

Typeset in Chaparral Pro Light 11/14pt by Integra Software Services Pvt. Ltd., Pondicherry, India

Printed in Italy by Printer Trento S.R.L.

A catalogue record for this title is available from the British Library

ISBN 9781471831997

Contents

The unseen poems

Introduction

This book has been designed to help you improve your skills and raise your achievement in the Eduqas GCSE English Literature Component 1 and Component 2 examinations.

How is the book structured?

The book is divided into two sections: the first section looks at all the poems in the WJEC Eduqas GCSE Anthology, and the second section supports the unseen poetry part of the exam. In the first section, there is an introductory section for each poem and a focus on the contexts of the poem. You will be able to work through the following stages to build your confidence and understanding of all the poems in the Anthology:

- **First thoughts** After reading through the poem for the first time you will think about your first impressions and reactions. What are your initial ideas about the poem? How do you respond to what you have read? Which questions would you like to ask about the poem?

- **Looking more closely at words and images** You will begin to focus more closely on the words, images and techniques used in the poem. You should now begin to annotate the poem in some detail, highlighting important features and making notes to help you understand the poem in more detail.

- **Looking more closely at structure and form** You will begin to focus more closely on the way the poem is organised. You should make notes to help you understand the form of the poem, the effect of rhythm and rhyme, and how this relates to the content.

- **Thinking about themes** You will focus on the main ideas and messages that the poet wants you to understand. In many poems there may be more than one theme, so you should be aware of alternate interpretations.

- **Developing an understanding of contexts** It is important to understand some of the contexts surrounding the poems. This could be social, historical or literary context, for example.

- **Developing your own individual response** It is important to understand and analyse how a poet uses language and techniques to create effects, but it is equally important to think about how the poem makes you feel. This section will help you consider your own thoughts and reactions to the poem.

- **Self-assessment** You will be given the opportunity to reflect upon your own understanding and how to improve it by completing a checklist.

- **Working on exam skills** You will look at an exam-style question for each poem and practise writing exam-style responses. You will have sample answers to annotate, evaluate and compare with your own work. There will be assessment criteria against which you can judge your performance and an opportunity for you to think about how to improve your performance.

- **Compare with...** You will find a list of poems that you might want to use for comparisons.

- **Approaching the examination** In this section you will work on techniques to improve your performance, focusing on how to plan, write and check your responses in timed conditions.

In the unseen poetry section you will learn to develop a considered individual response to poems you haven't studied before. You will be given the opportunity to reflect upon your own understanding and progress. There will be examples of exam-style questions and sample answers to assess, evaluate and compare with your own work.

The Poetry Anthology and the examination

What will I be asked to do in the exam?

The WJEC Eduqas Poetry Anthology is part of the assessment for Component 1 – Shakespeare and Poetry from 1789 to the present day.

Your response to poetry in this exam is assessed in Section B of Component 1. It is worth 40 marks and makes up 20 per cent of your final result for GCSE English Literature.

In this section you will be assessed on two poems from the WJEC Eduqas Poetry Anthology, and you should spend approximately one hour on your answer.

In the first question you will be asked to write about a specific poem from the Anthology. The whole poem will be printed on the exam paper. This question is worth 15 marks.

In the second question you will be asked to choose, write about and compare a second poem from the WJEC Eduqas Poetry Anthology. This question is worth 25 marks. Remember, it is important you choose an **appropriate** second poem.

For each poem you will be expected to consider the context of the poem, its content (what it is about), its theme (the key ideas) and the poet's use of language, structure and form.

You will need to study **all** of the poems in the WJEC Eduqas Poetry Anthology in order to prepare for this exam.

You will be assessed on Assessment Objectives AO1, AO2 and AO3 for these questions, and they are equally weighted in these questions.

You are **not** allowed to take a copy of the Poetry Anthology into the examination although the titles of the poems will be printed on the exam paper.

What do I need to know about this part of the exam?

The activities in this part of the book are to support your learning for the following section of the exam:
Component 1 Section B – Poetry from 1789 to the present day

Here are answers to some questions you may have about this part of the exam.

How much is this section worth?

This section is worth 20 per cent of your total mark.

How long should I spend on this section?

You should spend one hour on Section B.

Which Assessment Objectives are assessed in this section?

In Section B you will be assessed on AO1, AO2 and AO3.

Will I be able to use a copy of the Poetry Anthology in the exam?

No.

What will each question ask me to do?

You will have to answer both parts of the question: part (a) and part (b).

Part (a) is worth 15 marks and the marks are divided up like this: AO1 is worth 5 marks, AO2 is worth 5 marks and AO3 is worth 5 marks. In this part you will be given one poem from the Poetry Anthology to write about.

Part (b) is worth 25 marks and the marks are divided up like this: AO1 is worth 5 marks, AO2 is worth 10 marks and AO3 is worth 10 marks. In this part you will have to choose another poem from the Poetry Anthology and link it to the poem in part (a).

Will marks be allocated in this section for my accuracy in spelling, punctuation and the use of grammar?

No.

Will I need to study and learn about all the poems in the WJEC Eduqas Poetry Anthology?

Yes.

Remember, the titles of the poems will be printed on the exam paper but you won't be allowed to take the Anthology into the exam.

Assessment Objectives

What do they really mean? The simple truth!

Do not be worried when you hear your teachers talking about 'Assessment Objectives'. These are just the criteria or standards that will be used to assess your work.

When you study the poems in the WJEC Eduqas Poetry Anthology and when you write about poems that you have not previously studied for the unseen poetry section, you need to understand what the following Assessment Objectives are actually asking you to do.

AO1 asks you to give your own personal response to what you have read and how you show it.

AO1 says 'read, understand and respond to texts'. This just means that you will be reading the poems and showing that you understand them by saying what you think they are about and what some of the details mean.

AO1 says 'maintain a critical style and develop an informed personal response.' This means you need to think about what the poet wants to communicate and show how he/she does this.

AO1 says 'use textual reference, including quotes to support and illustrate interpretations'. For this you need to use evidence and examples from the poem to prove your points. You can quote by picking out words from the poem to support your opinions.

AO2 asks you to look at how language is used to create effects.

AO2 says 'analyse language, form and structure used by a writer to create meaning and effects'. It is probably easier to break this down and think about this objective in terms of three things:
- **Language** – write about the way the poet uses words, images and techniques to create effects.
- **Form** – this could be the type of poem the poet has chosen to write, such as a sonnet or a ballad, or his/her use of specific things like rhyme and rhythm.
- **Structure** – this is the way the poet has decided to organise his/her ideas. You could think about the way the poet has organised the whole poem or particular stanzas. Sometimes poems have a circular structure where the ending refers back to the first stanza.

AO2 says 'using subject terminology where appropriate'. Be careful not to treat this as a feature-spotting hunt! It is much more important to write about the effect the words have rather than to know the correct terminology, although you should use the terminology if you know it as you will be rewarded for using appropriate terminology as part of your answer.

AO3 is the objective about context.

AO3 says 'show understanding of relationships between texts and the contexts in which they were written'. Understanding the literary context of the poem is another important factor to consider. You do not need to become an expert on history. You just need to be able to do the following:
- Show that you understand how the poem is shaped or influenced by the period in which it was written.
- Show that you understand how the life and times of the poet may have influenced his/her writing.
- Show whether a modern reader would have a different viewpoint from that of someone in the period it was written.

Student-friendly marking criteria

Your teacher will show you the full marking criteria for the poetry responses in Section B in Component 1.

Here are the **key words** from the criteria so you can see at a glance what you need to do in order to move up the bands of assessment.

	AO1	AO2	AO3
Band 5 **13–15 marks**	Focus, overview, coherence, sensitive, evaluative, perceptive, originality, pertinent reference to text	Analyse, assured reference, explore, evaluate, precise terminology	Assured understanding of contexts
Band 4 **10–12 marks**	Focus, thoughtful, secure understanding, support and justify with well-chosen references	Discuss, thoughtful apt terminology	Secure understanding of contexts
Band 3 **7–9 marks**	Focus, general coherence, support and justify with appropriate references	Comment on, begin to write about, relevant terminology	Straightforward understanding of contexts
Band 2 **4–6 marks**	Some focus, some coherence, some understanding, some direct reference to the text	Point out and make simple comments, limited reference, some relevant terminology	Some understanding of contexts
Band 1 **1–3 marks**	Limited focus, occasional coherence, basic understanding, some general reference to text	Generalised comments, basic references, some terminology but not always accurate	Limited understanding of contexts

 TIP

Remember that, although 'comparison' is not written in the Assessment Objectives, you will be expected to make comparisons between the poems. As you work through the book, you will find activities that will remind you of this.

'The Manhunt' by Simon Armitage

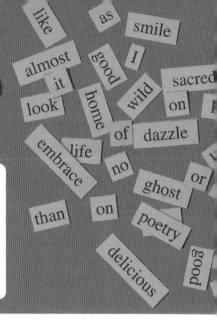

OBJECTIVES

▶ To explore and develop your response to 'The Manhunt' by Simon Armitage.

▶ To understand how Simon Armitage has used language, structure and form to present a relationship between partners.

▶ To understand some of the contexts of the poem.

Introduction

This poem is written in the first person, from the perspective of a wife whose husband has been seriously injured in war and has returned home. The poem focuses on how war can affect someone physically and mentally, and how it can affect relationships.

Simon Armitage is a modern poet who was born in West Yorkshire in 1963. He is a very successful poet who often writes about issues affecting society.

AO3 Context

This poem belongs to the collection called *The Not Dead,* which explores how soldiers and their families are affected by war and conflict. Sometimes referred to as 'Laura's Poem: The Manhunt', it is about a soldier who served in Bosnia as a peace keeper in the 1990s. He did not expect that he would be fighting on the mission but he was badly injured and discharged from the army because of his physical and psychological injuries.

AO1 First thoughts

ACTIVITY 1

(1) What are your initial thoughts about the poem's title, 'The Manhunt'? What is a manhunt usually associated with?

(2) Look at the first two lines of the poem. What do you think this poem might be about? Pick out words to prove this.

Glossary

porcelain – a delicate type of china

rudder – something used to steer a boat or ship

punctured – ruptured or pierced

foetus – an unborn child in the womb

 **Looking more closely at words and images**

ACTIVITY 2

1. The wife is tracing her finger along her husband's injuries. Pick out the verbs that are used to show her actions. What do you think these verbs suggest about her feelings?

2. Simon Armitage uses elaborate metaphors to describe the soldier's broken body and his injuries. Look at these metaphors: 'the frozen river which ran through his face'; 'the blown hinge of his lower jaw'. For each one write a few sentences explaining what you think Armitage means.

3. The soldier's collar bone is compared to 'damaged porcelain'. What do you think the poet is suggesting here? Do you think that this is an effective metaphor?

4. The soldier's 'punctured lung' is compared to 'parachute silk'. Why do you think the poet has used a metaphor associated with the military? Try to explain the points of comparison between the 'punctured lung' and 'parachute silk'.

5. The bullet or piece of shrapnel embedded in the soldier's body is described in quite a disturbing metaphor as 'the foetus of metal beneath his chest'. Why do you think the poet chose this image? Does it suggest anything about the relationship of the husband and wife now?

6. What does the metaphor 'the sweating unexploded mine buried deep in his mind' suggest about his experiences and the extent of his suffering?

AO2 Looking more closely at structure and form

ACTIVITY 3

1. The poem takes us through the wife's journey of trying to reconnect with her physically injured and emotionally traumatised husband. She is searching to find the man he once was before he went to war. Do you think that she is able to reconnect with her husband by the end of the poem? What does the line 'only then did I come close' suggest to you?

(2) When you read the poem aloud you will notice there is a slow rhythm. What technique does the poet use to create such a slow pace and rhythm? Do you think the poet is trying to suggest something about the soldier's healing process?

(3) The poem is written in a series of couplets. The rhyme scheme is not always regular, which makes it seem disjointed and fragmented. Why do you think the poet has deliberately created this effect?

Thinking about themes

 ACTIVITY 4

(1) The poem is not encouraging us to consider whether or not war is justified. Instead it focuses on the impact war has on relationships and the families of the soldiers. How does Armitage suggest that the relationship between the soldier and his wife has changed?

(2) Armitage presents the enduring strength of a relationship even in the most traumatic of circumstances. Pick out words/phrases from the poem that suggest this.

(3) One of the themes Armitage wants to show us is the damage that war can cause and the physical and mental effects of such a conflict. Try to explain how the image of 'his grazed heart' suggests both the physical and psychological suffering of the soldier.

 **Developing your own individual response**

 ACTIVITY 5

(1) What do you think the poet means by these lines?

> Only then could I bind the struts
> and climb the rungs of his broken ribs

(2) What do you think the line 'only then would he let me' suggests about the relationship between the soldier and his wife?

(3) There are several references to time in the poem. How many can you find? Why do you think the poet has repeatedly mentioned time?

(4) Think of four words to describe the effect this poem had on you.

> **! TIP**
>
> When you are choosing evidence from a poem, don't copy out large chunks, because many of the lines will not be relevant to the point you are making. Instead, be selective! Pick out a couple of words at a time and write about what they suggest and why they are effective. This technique will earn you more marks.

Self-assessment

 **ACTIVITY 6**

Answer true or false to the following statements.

I can comment on and find evidence for how Armitage:

- presents the relationship between the soldier and his wife
- uses metaphors to describe the physical and mental trauma of the soldier
- presents the effects of conflict.

Working on exam skills

 ACTIVITY 7

Look at this example of an exam-style question.

> How does Armitage write about relationships between partners in the poem?

- Write a section on language and imagery that you could include in your answer.
- Write a section on form and structure that you could include in your answer.

 TIPS

Remember to:
- make a clear point:
- use evidence from the poem to support your point:
- explain the effect of the evidence/quotations you have used:
- focus on particular word choices.

 ACTIVITY 8

This activity focuses on AO2. Read the following paragraph written by a student.

Armitage wants to emphasise the patience, care and loving devotion that the wife shows to her injured and damaged husband. He uses verbs to suggest her search to find and reconnect with her husband as she runs her finger along his body, noting his injuries. The verbs 'mind and attend' suggest the careful and gentle action of the wife as she touches and nurses his broken body. It could also imply that the wife is very patient in the way she deals with his psychological injuries. Some of the verbs, such as 'explore', 'finger' and 'thumb', seem quite tentative and could make us think that she is scared of hurting him. The verb 'trace' implies quite a slow movement which could also suggest that the physical healing will be a slow and drawn out process.

Find examples of where:
- this paragraph begins with a clear point
- the student uses evidence from the poem
- the student explains the effect of the quotations used
- the student focuses on particular word choices.

 ACTIVITY 9

After reading the sample answer, if you think you need to add anything to your paragraphs from Activity 7, redraft them now. For example, do you think you have included enough detail? Have you written about the effect of specific words?

Compare with…

'The Manhunt' could be compared with: 'Sonnet 43'; 'Valentine'; 'She Walks in Beauty'; 'Dulce et Decorum Est'; 'The Soldier'; 'Mametz Wood'.

'Sonnet 43' by Elizabeth Barrett Browning

OBJECTIVES

▶ To explore and develop your response to 'Sonnet 43' by Elizabeth Barrett Browning.

▶ To understand how Elizabeth Barrett Browning has used language, structure and form to present her feelings about love.

▶ To understand some of the contexts of the poem.

Introduction

This is an autobiographical poem written by Elizabeth Barrett Browning to her future husband, Robert Browning. In the poem, the poet describes the intensity of her love, which is powerful and all-encompassing.

Glossary

sonnet – a 14-line love poem with a regular rhyme scheme

ideal Grace – the Grace of God

quiet need – ordinary or simple need

AO3 Context

Elizabeth Barrett Browning eloped to Italy with Robert Browning to escape from her father's disapproval. She wrote this sonnet for Robert Browning before they were married, and it is part of a series of 44 sonnets called *Sonnets from the Portuguese* (published 1850). This title was based on his affectionate nickname for her, 'my little Portuguese', and these poems were a secret way for her to express her love for him.

AO1 First thoughts

📄 ACTIVITY 1

1. At the start of the poem the speaker asks the question, 'How do I love thee?' Count the number of different ways she loves Robert Browning.

2. The speaker repeats a particular phrase throughout the poem. What is the phrase, and how many times is it repeated? What do you think this suggests about the theme of the poem and the speaker's feelings?

3. Can you pick out any words connected with religion? What do you think these words suggest about the poet's feelings?

4. Although this is a very positive and beautiful poem, it does contain some negative words. Can you find any?

AO2 Looking more closely at words and images

📄 ACTIVITY 2

(1) Read lines 1 and 2 again. How does Elizabeth Barrett Browning measure her love here? Why do you think she has repeated the word 'and' in line 2?

(2) In lines 5 and 6, Barrett Browning describes her love in very different terms. What do you think she means when she says, 'to the level of every day's/Most quiet need'?

(3) Can you explain what she is suggesting about her love by using the words 'by sun and candle-light'?

(4) How does Barrett Browning describe her love in lines 7 and 8? What do you think she means when she uses the words 'freely' and 'purely'?

(5) In lines 9 to 12, Barrett Browning compares the intensity of her love with the intensity she felt for religion when she was a child. What do the words 'old griefs' and 'my lost saints' suggest about her previous experiences in life? Do you learn anything about Barrett Browning's religious faith here?

(6) Read the final two lines of the sonnet. What do the nouns 'breath, Smiles, tears' imply about her love?

AO2 Looking more closely at structure and form

📄 ACTIVITY 3

(1) This poem is written in the form of a traditional Petrarchan sonnet. Lines 1–8 form the octave which sets out the theme of the poem. Lines 9–14 form the sestet. What aspects of love do you think these lines focus on?

(2) Why do you think Barrett Browning has used enjambment in these lines?

> I love thee to the level of every day's
>
> Most quiet need, by sun and candle-light

(3) The sonnet is written in iambic pentameter, with five unstressed and five stressed syllables in each line. What effect do you think Barrett Browning wanted to achieve by doing this?

4. In lines 3 and 4, the long 'e' vowel sound is used in the words 'reach', 'feeling', 'Being' and 'Ideal'. What effect do you think is created by this technique?

5. The sonnet begins with a question which Barrett Browning answers throughout the course of the next 14 lines. What effect does the poet want this question to have on the reader?

6. In the final line Barrett Browning says, 'I shall but love thee better after death'. Why do you think she places this 'way' at the end of the sonnet?

Thinking about themes

ACTIVITY 4

1. Barrett Browning intends to show the reader that love can be a powerful, intense and ultimately uplifting force. Do you agree or disagree? Pick out words and phrases from the poem to back up your own view.

2. What does Barrett Browning suggest about the nature of love by identifying so many different kinds of love in the poem?

3. In the line 'I love thee with a love I seemed to lose/With my lost saints', the poet seems to suggest her loss of religious faith. Can you find any words or phrases to suggest that Barrett Browning is not totally without faith?

AO1 Developing your own individual response

 ## ACTIVITY 5

(1) Why do you think capital letters have been used for the words 'Being', 'Ideal', 'Grace', 'Right' and 'Proud'?

(2) The poem describes the intensity of feelings that love can cause and the many different ways in which Barrett Browning loves. However, she doesn't mention the physical side of love. Why do you think this is?

(3) Which one of all the 'ways' that she loves him do you consider to be the most important? Explain your choice by referring to the poem.

(4) Has the poem changed the way in which you think about love? Explain why or why not. Remember to refer to the poem in your answer.

> **! TIP**
>
> You will score higher marks if you write about a poem in detail and discuss its ideas thoughtfully. Giving your own critical stance on the poem will also be rewarded.

Self-assessment

 ## ACTIVITY 6

Answer true or false to the following statements.

I can comment on and find evidence for how:

- Barrett Browning uses language to communicate her feelings about love
- Barrett Browning uses structure and form to present her ideas
- the sonnet relates to the context in which it was written.

Working on exam skills

 ACTIVITY 7

Look at this example of an exam-style question.

> How does Elizabeth Barrett Browning write about love in the poem?

- Write a paragraph or two that you could include in your answer about how the poet uses language to convey her ideas.
- Write a section on form and structure that you could include in your answer.

 ACTIVITY 8

Now read the following paragraph written by a student.

Elizabeth Barrett Browning presents love as a powerful and all-consuming force that helps her to reach impossible limits. For example, she writes that she loves 'to the depth and breadth and height/My soul can reach'. This example of a metaphor linked with space suggests that love is something that completely fills her soul. The repetition of the word 'and' here also implies that perhaps the way that love affects her is an endless list. Furthermore the repetition might suggest that Barrett Browning is excited and breathless when describing how deeply and passionately she feels for her lover. She uses positive language to convince her lover about how deeply she loves him.

Find examples of where:

- this paragraph begins with a clear point
- the student uses evidence from the poem
- the student explains the effect of the quotations used
- the student focuses on particular word choices.

Is there anything you would do to improve or add to this sample answer?

 ACTIVITY 9

After reading the sample answer, if you think you need to add anything to your paragraphs from Activity 7, redraft them now.

Compare with...
'Sonnet 43' could be compared with: 'The Manhunt'; 'Valentine'; 'She Walks in Beauty'; 'Cozy Apologia'.

'London' by William Blake

OBJECTIVES

▶ To explore and develop your response to 'London' by William Blake.
▶ To understand how William Blake has used language, structure and form to present his view of London.
▶ To understand some of the contexts of the poem.

In this poem the poet, William Blake, is walking through the streets of London, making a note of what he sees around him.

Introduction

William Blake was born in London in 1757. In 1794 Blake published two collections of poems, called *The Songs of Innocence* and *The Songs of Experience*. *The Songs of Innocence* are about childhood, nature and love and so the tone is positive and optimistic. However, *The Songs of Experience* were written as a contrast and they show the damaging and negative effects that the modern, industrialised life had on nature and people. 'London' is taken from *The Songs of Experience*, and the tone is dark and disturbing.

AO3 Context

Blake was disillusioned with authority and industrialisation, as ordinary people were controlled by landlords and institutions. In his poem 'London', he is perhaps suggesting that such poor living conditions could inspire a revolution and change on the streets of his own capital city. Although a religious man, Blake was critical of the Church of England because he felt that the established Church was not doing enough to help the children of London, who were forced to work in dangerous and terrible conditions.

In 1789, the ordinary people of France rebelled against the royalty and aristocracy of the country and overthrew those in power. This rebellion was known as the French Revolution. People had become frustrated with the king and his inability to deal with dreadful living conditions, food shortages and the financial situation of the country. The French king and queen, Louis XVI and Marie Antoinette, were among those executed.

Glossary

thro' – through
charter'd – charted or mapped
Thames – the river flowing through London
woe – sorrow or misfortune
manacles – chains or handcuffs
appalls – fills with horror
hapless – unlucky
harlot – prostitute
blights – spoils or ruins
hearse – a vehicle for carrying a coffin to a funeral

After the Revolution, a new government was created to represent the people and to run the country.

William Blake supported this rebellion because he was unhappy with the living conditions, child labour and exploitation that he could see around him.

AO1 First thoughts

 ACTIVITY 1

1. Look back over the whole poem. Pick out all the words that are negative and that make you think of danger, sadness or cruelty.

2. In the first stanza Blake has repeated the words 'charter'd' and 'marks'. Why do you think he does this? What effect does the repetition of the words create?

3. Read the final stanza again. In this stanza things that should be associated with joy and happiness are linked with sadness, grief and death. Find two examples of this.

4. The poem is structured so that each stanza focuses on a different aspect of London. Why do you think Blake writes about different 'snapshots' of the city and the people who live there?

AO2 Looking more closely at words and images

 ACTIVITY 2

1. In the second stanza Blake writes about the 'mind-forg'd manacles'. Why is he suggesting that the people of London are imprisoned and in chains? Can you explain why the manacles are 'mind-forg'd'?

2. In the third stanza Blake writes about a 'Chimney-sweeper' and a 'hapless Soldier'. What do you think Blake is suggesting about these people?

3. In the same stanza Blake turns his attention to the 'black'ning Church' and the 'Palace walls'. What do you think he is trying to suggest about these places?

4. Why do you think Blake repeats the word 'every' so many times in the poem?

AO2 Looking more closely at structure and form

 ACTIVITY 3

1. If you read the poem aloud you will notice that it has a steady beat or rhythm, and a regular rhyme scheme with repetition. This will perhaps suggest to the reader that it sounds like a song. Why do you think Blake does this?

2. Why do you think Blake has organised his poem so that all the stanzas are the same length?

3. In the final stanza, Blake writes about a 'new-born Infant' and the 'Marriage hearse'. What is Blake trying to tell the reader here? Why do you think he decided to finish his poem with these images?

4. Blake uses heavy vowel sounds in the word 'woe' and the long sounds in 'cry' and 'sigh'. What do you think he is trying to tell us about the lives of the people by doing this?

Thinking about themes

 ACTIVITY 4

1. Some people feel the ideas in the poem are quite political and that Blake is protesting about the conditions in the city. Can you find a quote from the text to support this?

2. Are you able to work out how Blake felt about the Church and religion at this time? Can you find a quote from the poem to support this?

3. Some people think that the poem presents a bleak and pessimistic view of the city with little hope for the future. Do you agree or disagree with this? Use a quote from the poem to back up your view.

AO1 Developing your own individual response

 ACTIVITY 5

In this poem Blake is writing about the conditions he witnesses and the instances of human suffering around him. Some people think it is a negative and upsetting poem.

How do you respond to it? Use examples from the poem to support your ideas.

 TIP

When you are writing about the poet, don't refer to him/her by the first name – he/she isn't your best friend! Instead say 'William Blake suggests…' or 'Blake tells us that…'.

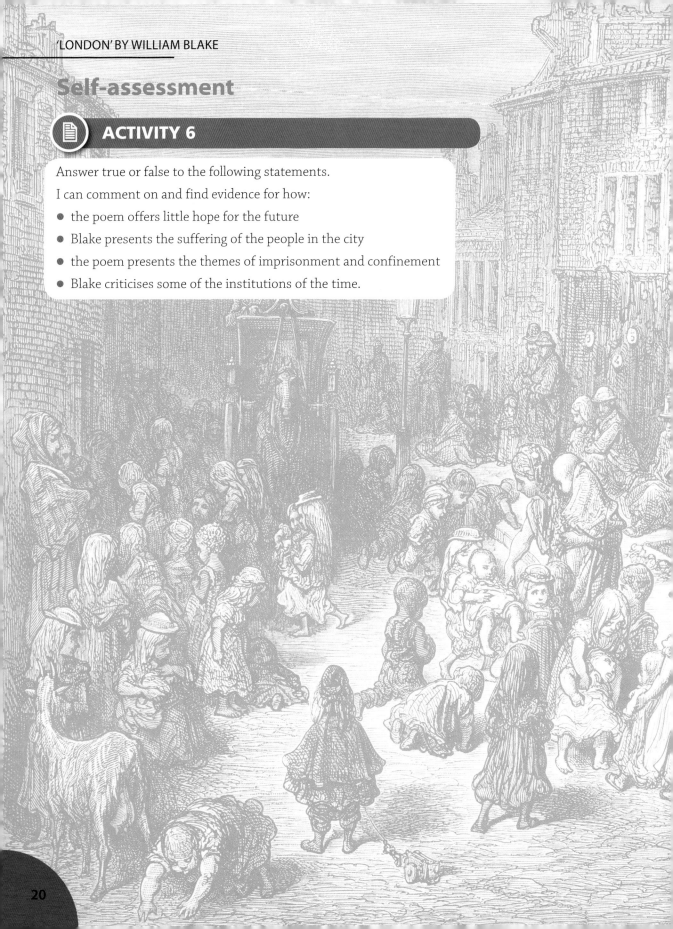

Self-assessment

ACTIVITY 6

Answer true or false to the following statements.

I can comment on and find evidence for how:

- the poem offers little hope for the future
- Blake presents the suffering of the people in the city
- the poem presents the themes of imprisonment and confinement
- Blake criticises some of the institutions of the time.

Working on exam skills

 ACTIVITY 7

Look at this example of an exam-style question.

> Write about the ways Blake presents the city in this poem.

Choose three quotations from those listed below and use them to write three paragraphs in which you:

- comment on the way the poet has used language, form and structure to create meaning and effect
- show you understand how the poem reflects the poet's attitudes to society.

> I wander thro' each charter'd street,
> Near where the charter'd Thames does flow
>
> In every voice, in every ban,
> The mind-forg'd manacles I hear:
>
> How the Chimney-sweeper's cry
> Every black'ning Church appalls,
>
> How the youthful Harlot's curse
> Blasts the new-born Infant's tear
> And blights with plagues the Marriage hearse.

 ACTIVITY 8

When you have finished, read the following paragraph written by a student.

> Blake expresses his feelings of horror as he wanders 'thro' each charter'd street'. He clearly feels that the people in the city are powerless against the wealthy landlords. This is suggested by the use of the word 'charter'd', which makes us think of restriction and confinement. Blake goes on to repeat the word in the next line in connection with the river, 'near where the charter'd Thames does flow'. We usually think of rivers as being natural and free-flowing, but Blake seems to feel that even nature itself is restricted and suffering from oppression, just like the people.

Find examples of where:

- this paragraph begins with a clear point
- the student uses evidence from the poem
- the student explains the effect of the quotations used
- the student focuses on particular word choices.

 ACTIVITY 9

Now compare what you have written with this sample answer. If you need to add anything to your answers to Activity 7, redraft them.

Compare with...

'London' could be compared with: 'The Prelude'; 'To Autumn'; 'Living Space'.

'The Soldier' by Rupert Brooke

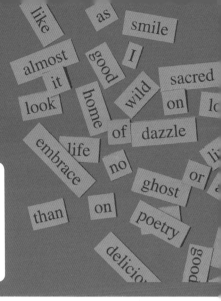

OBJECTIVES

▶ To explore and develop your response to 'The Soldier' by Rupert Brooke.
▶ To understand how Rupert Brooke has used language, structure and form to express his feelings about war and death.
▶ To understand some of the contexts of the poem.

Introduction

This poem was written in 1914 at the start of World War I. Rupert Brooke talks about the soldier's possible death and the peaceful afterlife he will enjoy after sacrificing himself for his country.

Brooke himself fought in World War I and died in 1915 from blood poisoning after suffering a mosquito bite. After his death, Brooke came to represent the tragic loss of talented young men during the war.

Glossary

bore – created
roam – travel/wander
blest – blessed

AO3 Context

At the beginning of World War I people were idealistic and naïve about war, seeing it as something noble and heroic. Perhaps this is understandable because no previous war had ever involved mustard gas, trench warfare, planes and machine guns. World War I was in fact a bloody, brutal and destructive war with over 20 million lives lost on both sides. The world changed forever as a result of this war.

Brooke's poems about war and death are quite romanticised and optimistic perhaps because they were written before people were really aware of the senseless slaughter and futility of battle. When you study 'Dulce et Decorum Est' by Wilfred Owen, you will immediately notice a more bitter and violent tone, as that poem was written in 1917 during the height of the horrors of World War I.

 **First thoughts**

 **ACTIVITY 1**

1. From whose point of view do you think the poem is written? Can you find evidence to prove this?

2. What does the poem seem to be telling us about attitudes to war? Can you find a word from the poem to back up your opinion?

AO2 Looking more closely at words and images

ACTIVITY 2

1. If the soldier dies in war and is buried, how does he think his body will change 'some corner of a foreign field' into a place that is 'forever England'?

2. How do you think the narrator views death? Find evidence from the poem to prove this.

3. Which words does Brooke use to describe England in the first stanza? What impression do you think he wants to create of his country?

4. Copy and complete this list of all the words you can find in the poem that are connected with war and death and those that are connected with peace and rest. What do you think this suggests about the tone and purpose of the poem?

Words connected with war/death	Words connected with peace/rest
die	rich earth

5. The narrator describes his body as 'A body of England's'. What do you think he means by this?

6. Read the second stanza carefully. What view of heaven does the narrator have? Find words from the poem to back up your ideas. Do you think the narrator's view of England is different from or similar to his view of heaven? Find a few quotes to support your opinions.

AO2 Looking more closely at structure and form

 **ACTIVITY 3**

(1) This poem is written in the form of a sonnet, which is a form of writing often associated with love poetry. Why do you think Brooke chose to use this form of poetry when writing 'The Soldier'?

(2) Read the opening two lines of each stanza again. Do you notice that one word appears in both openings? Why do you think the narrator does this, and whom do you think he is addressing?

(3) Do you think there is a shift in focus between stanzas 1 and 2? What do you think is the main focus of each stanza? Find words from the poem to support your opinions.

Thinking about themes

ACTIVITY 4

(1) Read the following statements about the poem and decide whether you agree or disagree with them. Find words or phrases from the poem to back up your opinion.
- The poem idealises and romanticises war.
- This poem is a piece of propaganda to encourage people to fight for their country.
- The poem is not a war poem: it is a celebration of patriotism.
- This poem is excessively sentimental and unrealistic.

(2) How many references can you find in the poem to the words 'English' or 'England'? Why do you think the narrator has repeated this idea so often? How do you think this feeling of patriotism helps the narrator deal with his own mortality?

AO1 Developing your own individual response

 ACTIVITY 5

(1) Why do you think Rupert Brooke chose 'The Soldier' as his title instead of 'A Soldier'?

(2) Brooke uses several different ideas to describe England. Below is one student's mind map about these ideas and their effects. Think about and discuss these ideas, and add some of your own.

(3) Do you consider 'The Soldier' to be a pro-war or anti-war poem, or neither? Explain your response by referring to details from the poem.

(4) Has the poem changed the way in which you think about war and death? Explain your opinion by referring to details from the poem.

> **! TIP**
>
> Make sure you write about the whole poem – sometimes students focus too much on one part and never reach the end!

Self-assessment

ACTIVITY 6

Answer true or false to the following statements.

I can comment on and find evidence for how:

- Brooke uses language to communicate his feelings about war and death
- Brooke uses structure and form to present his ideas
- the poem relates to the context in which it was written.

Working on exam skills

 ACTIVITY 7

Look at this example of an exam-style question:

> Consider how Rupert Brooke writes about war in the poem 'The Soldier'. Use examples from the poem to support your answer.

Write a section on language that could be included in your answer.

 ACTIVITY 8

Now read the following paragraph written by a student.

> Rupert Brooke presents war as something honourable and idealised because he doesn't focus on the bloodshed and horror of fighting, nor on the grief felt by the families at home. The sonnet begins with the words 'If I should die', and some people might feel that the soldier is in fact being realistic by mentioning death and confronting an issue people don't usually want to think about. This suggests the soldier is facing his mortality, although he is clearly not afraid of death as he sees it as just the beginning for his everlasting life in heaven, 'breathing English air'.

Find examples of where:

- the paragraph begins with a clear point
- the student uses evidence from the poem
- the student writes about the effectiveness of language.

Think about what you could do to add to this sample answer.

 ACTIVITY 9

Now write a section about your own individual response to this poem.

Compare with...

'The Soldier' could be compared with: 'Dulce et Decorum Est'; 'Mametz Wood'; 'As Imperceptibly as Grief'; 'The Manhunt'.

'She Walks in Beauty' by Lord Byron (George Gordon)

▶ To develop your response to 'She Walks in Beauty' by Lord Byron.
▶ To understand how Byron uses language, structure and form to communicate his feelings of awe and admiration.
▶ To understand some of the contexts of the poem.

Introduction

In this poem, Byron describes how he was struck by the unusual beauty of a woman he met at a ball. She was in mourning and wearing a black dress set with glistening spangles that caught Byron's attention and inspired him to write the poem.

AO3 Context

Lord Byron (George Gordon) wrote in the early nineteenth century, during the Romantic period. Romantic poets did not necessarily write about love but they were part of a movement that turned against the obsession with order and rationality of the eighteenth century. They placed a greater emphasis on emotions and the importance of individual thoughts and personal feelings. Romantic writers experimented with form, style and content, and not only with poetry – the novel as a genre also became more important.

Byron had a notorious reputation because of his wild behaviour and many affairs with women and men. Allegedly he was rumoured to have abused his wife, had affairs with actresses and an incestuous affair with his sister. Perhaps understandably he was regarded as 'mad, bad and dangerous to know'! His reputation grew so scandalous that he was forced to leave Britain and move to Europe, where he caught a fever and died in 1824.

Glossary

climes – countries
aspect – features
mellowed – softened
impaired – spoiled/ruined
tress – lock of hair
o'er – over
eloquent – expressive

AO1 First thoughts

ACTIVITY 1

1. What do you think is the stereotypical image of beauty in today's society?
2. What do we find out about the physical appearance of the woman in the poem?

(3) What is the narrator's attitude to the woman? Find evidence to prove your answer.

AO2 Looking more closely at words and images

ACTIVITY 2

(1) What do you think the title 'She Walks in Beauty' suggests about the qualities of this woman?

(2) Byron uses many words and images associated with darkness and light. List as many of them as you can in a table like this, and try to explain the effect of these words.

Quote	Effect created
Like the night / Of cloudless climes and starry skies	Suggests her beauty is unusual
	Suggests a clear, beautiful and flawless complexion
	Suggests her personality and conscience are as clear as a clear, cloudless sky

(3) What do you think Byron means when he writes:

> One shade the more, one ray the less,
>
> Had half impaired the nameless grace
>
> Which waves in every raven tress.

(4) In the second stanza, the poet uses the words 'softly', 'serenely sweet' and 'dear' to describe the woman. Annotate these words to show all the possible connotations they create in your mind. Remember to consider the sounds of the words as well.

(5) Read the final stanza again and pick out the words that show the narrator's admiration for the woman.

AO2 Looking more closely at structure and form

 **ACTIVITY 3**

1. Each stanza is made up of six lines, and there is a regular rhyme scheme in each one. Why do you think the poet has chosen to create such a steady rhythm? In what way might this relate to the content of the poem?

2. The lines of the poem are written in iambic tetrameter, which is commonly used in the writing of hymns. Why do you think Byron has adopted this form? What do you think it suggests about his feelings for the woman in the poem?

Thinking about themes

 **ACTIVITY 4**

1. One of the themes of the poem is appearance. In how many different ways does Byron say she is beautiful? In describing her 'raven tress' and describing her as 'like the night', Byron seems to be going against the conventional standards of beauty for the time. What do you think he is suggesting about beauty?

2. Byron emphasises the purity and innocence of the woman. Why do you think he stresses her goodness as well as her beauty? Why do you think Byron chose to end the poem with a comment on her virtue and innocence?

3. Do you think that Byron is in love with this woman? Or do you think that he simply feels a sense of awe and admiration for the unnamed woman? Refer to words in the poem when you explain your opinion.

AO1 Developing your own individual response

 **ACTIVITY 5**

Students have written the following comments in response to this poem. Select two points that you agree with and two that you disagree with. For each, find words or evidence from the poem to support the view.

Student A

Byron is objectifying the woman by breaking her down into bodily parts when he describes her — what her eyes are like, how she walks, etc.

Student B

The poet presents the woman as something ideal and unobtainable. He is clearly idealising her by comparing her beauty to things so vast and universal that her beauty seems almost out of this world.

Student C

It is obvious that Byron just wants to seduce her!

Student D

Although the poet writes in detail about her outer appearance, he also acknowledges that she has 'thoughts' and an inner life that he cannot access.

Student E

Byron isn't in love with this woman ... he is simply showing his admiration and appreciation for perfection and beauty.

Self-assessment

 ACTIVITY 6

Answer true or false to the following statements.

I can comment on and find evidence for how Byron:

- uses language to describe the woman
- presents his attitude to the woman.

 TIP

Remember to show that you are aware of the context surrounding the poem. For example, does the poem suggest how women were viewed and treated at this time in society? Does the poem tell us anything about what was considered to be ideal qualities of a woman at the time?

Working on exam skills

 ACTIVITY 7

Look at this example of an exam-style question.

> How does Byron show his feelings of admiration in 'She Walks in Beauty'?

Choose three of the quotations below and use them to write three short paragraphs in which you:

- respond to the task by giving your own individual thoughts
- look closely at the language, words and images used.

> She walks in beauty, like the night
> Of cloudless climes and starry skies
>
> And all that's best of dark and bright
> Meet in her aspect and her eyes
>
> Where thoughts serenely sweet express,
> How pure, how dear their dwelling place
>
> And on that cheek, and o'er that brow,
> So soft, so calm, yet eloquent,
> The smiles that win, the tints that glow
>
> A mind at peace with all below,
> A heart whose love is innocent!

 ACTIVITY 8

Annotate your paragraphs to show where you have:

- made a clear point
- used evidence from the poem
- explained the effect of the quotations used
- focused on particular word choices.

 ACTIVITY 9

Now look at the Assessment Objectives on page 6.

- Which criteria do you think you have demonstrated in your answer?
- What do you think you need to do to improve your performance?

Compare with…

'She Walks in Beauty' could be compared with: 'The Manhunt'; 'Sonnet 43'; 'Valentine'; 'To Autumn'.

'Living Space' by Imtiaz Dharker

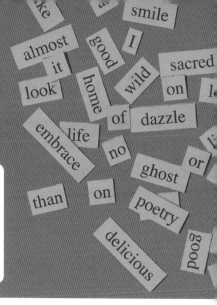

OBJECTIVES

▸ To explore and develop your response to 'Living Space' by Imtiaz Dharker.
▸ To understand how Imtiaz Dharker has used language, structure and form to present her feelings about a place.
▸ To understand some of the contexts of the poem.

Introduction

Imtiaz Dharker was born in Pakistan and brought up in Scotland, and her poetry often focuses on subjects such as religion, faith and culture. In this poem she is writing about poverty and living conditions in the shanty towns and slum areas of Mumbai (Bombay) in India.

AO3 Context

Mumbai is home to 22 million people, and 70 per cent of these people live in slums. Asia's largest slum is located in Mumbai, where there is limited access to electricity, clean water, food or opportunities for education. Many of the inhabitants of the slums are second-generation residents whose parents moved there many years ago to look for work. In these areas, there is tremendous poverty with unending stretches of narrow dirty lanes and overcrowded communal bathroom facilities. Huts are small, cramped and overcrowded, and the open sewers often contaminate sources of clean drinking water.

AO1 First thoughts

ACTIVITY 1

1. What are your first thoughts about the title, 'Living Space'?
2. What do you find out about the living conditions in this area from reading the first stanza?
3. Write a list of all the words associated with light and dark in the poem.

Glossary

vertical – straight
miraculous – beyond rational explanation

33

AO2 Looking more closely at words and images

📄 ACTIVITY 2

(1) What do you think the poet is suggesting about the living conditions when she writes that 'Beams / balance crookedly' and 'The whole structure leans dangerously'? What do you think this is suggesting about the inhabitants' experience of life?

(2) The poet uses the technique of personification in the line, 'Nails clutch at open seams'. What image do you think the poet wants to create in our minds?

(3) In the second stanza the poet describes the eggs in a wire basket as 'fragile curves of white'. What qualities does she notice about the eggs? What else do you think this idea of fragility could refer to in the poem? Explain your ideas.

(4) How many references are there to religion and faith in the poem? Make a list of them.

(5) Annotate the following quotes with your thoughts and feelings about the words, and what they suggest to you.

Into this rough frame,
someone has squeezed
a living space.

Hung out over the dark edge
of a slanted universe
the bright, thin walls of faith.

AO2 Looking more closely at structure and form

 **ACTIVITY 3**

(1) Throughout the poem Imtiaz Dharker often uses enjambment, and she also breaks up the rhythm of the lines. Look for examples of where you think she does this and decide what effect you think she was hoping to achieve.

(2) Dharker has created three stanzas of varying length. Why do you think she has done this, and what do you think she was trying to tell us about her feelings?

(3) Stanza two is made up of only three lines. Try to explain why you think Dharker has done this. How do you think the structure of this stanza reflects the content of the poem?

(4) There is no regular rhyme pattern in this poem although some words do rhyme. Write a list of the rhyming words and think about what this irregular rhyme pattern might suggest about the poet's feelings.

Thinking about themes

 **ACTIVITY 4**

(1) The fragility and precariousness of the homes in the poem could be seen as a metaphor. Can you work out what Dharker might be trying to tell us about life and existence?

(2) What do you think Dharker is suggesting about the theme of religion in the final line of the poem? What do you think will happen to the eggs?

(3) Do you think the message of the poem is essentially optimistic or pessimistic? Explain your viewpoint by referring to the poem.

AO1 Developing your own individual response

 **ACTIVITY 5**

(1) Draw a mind map to show what you consider to be the main points and most effective images of the poem.

(2) What do you think this poem has taught you about different ways of life? In which ways has the poem made you think about your own lifestyle? Refer to words from the poem to back up your ideas.

What do you consider to be the five most important words in the poem? Explain your reasons for your choices.

 Think of four words to describe the effect the poem had on you.

! TIP

When you are selecting words from a poem and using quotes, it is always more effective if you integrate the quote neatly into your sentence instead of writing the quote at the end of the line. For example, 'The person who had "dared to place" the eggs in the basket was clearly hopeful and optimistic that the "fragile curves of white" would remain intact.'

Self-assessment

 ACTIVITY 6

Answer true or false to the following statements.

I can comment on and find evidence for how:

- Dharker presents the living condition in the slums of Mumbai
- Dharker uses language, structure and form to describe her feelings about the place
- the poem relates to the context in which it was written.

Working on exam skills

 ACTIVITY 7

Read this paragraph, written in response to the task:

> How does Imtiaz Dharker create a sense of place in the poem?

Dharker immediately creates a sense of chaos about the slum area ← a clear point
that she is describing. The word 'problem' suggests that she is unhappy ← evidence to support the point
about the conditions she sees, and the fact that the 'beams balance crookedly'
makes me think that the buildings are unstable, old and so precarious that
they could collapse at any moment. Dharker notices that 'nails clutch at open ← integrated quotes
seams' and this, to me, makes the reader feel that just like the buildings, the
people themselves are clinging on to life by a thread that could so easily be
broken. The fact that the poet uses personification to describe the buildings
('balance', 'clutch', 'leans') seems to emphasise that the buildings and the
inhabitants are in the same condition. ← explanation of quotes/ close focus on language

 ACTIVITY 8

Write a paragraph giving your own response to the task in Activity 7, but focusing on form and structure.

You might want to look at the sample response above to give you an idea of how to structure your answer.

 ACTIVITY 9

Now annotate your own paragraph from Activity 8. If you think you have forgotten to include anything in your paragraph, add it in.

Look at the criteria for AO2 on p. 5 and try to decide which band your paragraph would fit into.

Compare with…
'Living Space' could be compared with: 'London'; 'The Prelude'.

'As Imperceptibly as Grief' by Emily Dickinson

like as smile almost good I it home wild sacr look of dazzle embrace life no ghost than on poetry delicious good

OBJECTIVES

▶ To explore and develop your response to 'As Imperceptibly as Grief' by Emily Dickinson.

▶ To understand how Emily Dickinson has used language, structure and form to present her feelings about the passing of time.

▶ To understand some of the contexts of the poem.

Introduction

In this poem, Emily Dickinson is writing about her initial regret about the passing of time and the changing of the seasons.

AO3 Context

Emily Dickinson was born in 1830 and raised in a strict Puritan household in Massachusetts in New England, America. She became a reclusive woman who did not leave her home for nearly 30 years! Many of her poems were inspired by nature and, like 'As Imperceptibly as Grief', they often focus on the passing of time. This poem was written around 1850, but along with all her other work was only published posthumously in 1886.

AO1 First thoughts

Glossary

imperceptibly – gradually/subtly

lapsed away – fell away/ passed away

perfidy – betrayal/ disloyalty

distilled – let fall in drops

sequestered – set apart/ removed

courteous – polite

harrowing – distressing/ deeply upsetting

thus – so

keel – a boat

ACTIVITY 1

(1) What are your first thoughts about the title of the poem? What do you think the poem is going to be about?

(2) Read the poem aloud. What sort of tone of voice do you think is most suitable? Experiment and decide whether you think it should be read in an anxious, angry, melancholic or resigned way, for example. Pick out any words that you think could give you clues about how to read it.

(3) Underline five words which you think have positive associations, and five words which seem more negative.

AO2 Looking more closely at words and images

 **ACTIVITY 2**

1. The first stanza describes how the season of summer is gradually changing. Pick out the words and phrases that suggest how the poet feels about this change. What mood is created in this opening stanza, and how do you think the poet achieves this?

2. In the second stanza, find examples of where the poet has personified nature. Try to explain why you think she has done this.

3. Why do you think the poet has compared summer to a 'guest who would be gone'? What might this suggest about her feelings?

4. In the final stanza, the poet suggests the passing of time is unlike the movement of a bird or a boat. Try to explain why you think she does this.

5. Do you think the tone of the poem changes between the first and final stanzas? Pick out some words and phrases that might suggest a change in the poet's feelings.

6. Why do you think the poet refers to summer as 'Our summer'? What effect do you think this has on the reader?

AO2 Looking more closely at structure and form

ACTIVITY 3

1. What effect do the words 'Sequestered', 'distilled', 'imperceptibly' and 'perfidy' have on your reading of the poem?

2. Draw a mind map to show how the season gradually changes throughout the poem. Select one key word or phrase from each stanza to represent the change.

3. There is no particular rhyme scheme in the poem. Why do you think this is?

Thinking about themes

 ACTIVITY 4

Students have made the following comments about the themes of the poem. Read each one and decide whether or not you agree with the comments. Remember to find evidence from the poem to back up your own ideas.

Student A

The passing of summer and the gradual changing of the seasons could be symbolic of the poet gradually losing her own happiness and sliding into a period of darkness.

Student B

Although the poem is about regret and the loss of summer, the poem is also a celebration of nature as the poet comes to appreciate the beauty of the seasons.

Student C

The poem is essentially about change ... a change in the seasons, a change in the days and, most importantly, a change in the feelings of the poet herself.

AO1 Developing your own individual response

 ACTIVITY 5

(1) How do you think Dickinson wants the reader to respond to the poem? What is your response and how has this response been created by the poet? You might want to select your answer from the options in this list or to choose your own ideas. Choose words or phrases from the poem to support your ideas.

sadness	indifference	anger	despair
reflection	thoughtfulness	admiration	disappointment

(2) Some people have found the last two lines of the poem to be rather enigmatic (mysterious). What is your reaction to them?

(3) Has the poem changed the way in which you think about the passing of time? Explain why or why not. Remember to refer to words from the poem in your answer.

 TIP

You can score high marks if you find well-chosen quotes from the poem to support your points.

Self-assessment

 ACTIVITY 6

Answer true or false to the following statements.

I can comment on and find evidence for how:

- Dickinson uses language to communicate her feelings about the passing of time
- Dickinson presents her ideas about nature
- the poem relates to some of the contexts in which it was written.

Working on exam skills

 ACTIVITY 7

Look at this example of an exam-style question.

> How does Emily Dickinson write about her feelings in this poem?

Choose three of the quotations below and use them to write three short paragraphs in which you:

- respond to the task by giving your thoughts about how her feelings have been presented in these lines
- look closely at the language, words and images used.

> As imperceptibly as grief
> The summer lapsed away
>
> The dusk drew earlier in,
> The morning foreign shone,
>
> A courteous, yet harrowing grace,
> As guest who would be gone.
>
> Our summer made her light escape
> Into the beautiful.

 ACTIVITY 8

Annotate your paragraphs to show where you have:

- made a clear point
- used evidence from the poem
- explained the effect of the quotations used
- focused on particular word choices.

 ACTIVITY 9

Now look at the Assessment Objectives on p. 5.

- Which criteria do you think you have shown in your answer?
- What do you think you need to do to improve your performance?

Compare with...

'As Imperceptibly as Grief' could be compared with: 'To Autumn'; 'The Prelude'; 'Afternoons'.

'Cozy Apologia' by Rita Dove

OBJECTIVES

▶ To explore and develop your response to 'Cozy Apologia' by Rita Dove.
▶ To understand how Dove uses language, structure and form to explore relationships.
▶ To understand some of the contexts of the poem.

Introduction

In this autobiographical poem, Rita Dove expresses her love for her husband, Fred.

AO3 Context

Rita Dove is the youngest ever US Poet Laureate and the first African American to hold the position. This poem, written in 2003, refers to her struggle with society's opinion about whom she should love. Dove is of African American descent while her husband, Fred, is of pure German descent.

'Big Bad Floyd' refers to Hurricane Floyd, a powerful storm that ripped along the Atlantic coast in 1999, killing many people and causing $6 billion worth of damage.

AO1 First thoughts

ACTIVITY 1

1. What does the word 'cozy' make you think of? What do you think this suggests about the atmosphere of the poem?
2. The poem is written in the first person. How does this affect your response as a reader?

Glossary

cozy – American spelling of 'cosy'

exudes – oozes/pours out

drying matte – drying to a dull finish

dappled mare – horse with a mottled/spotted coat

furrowed brow – wrinkled forehead

reminiscences – memories

sissy – girly/womanish

cussing up – blowing up

aerie – a bird's nest on a cliff or mountaintop

melancholy – sadness

AO2 Looking more closely at words and images

ACTIVITY 2

1. In the first line, the poet writes 'I could pick anything and think of you'. What does this tell the reader about her feelings for her husband?

2. In the first stanza, pick out all the words the poet uses to suggest that she sees her husband as a heroic figure. What do you think this suggests about how she views their relationship?

3. Look at the opening lines of the stanza. What is the poet's attitude to modern society? Select words from the poem to support your ideas.

4. The hurricane causes her to reminisce about relationships she had when she was younger. How do you think she feels about these relationships now that she is older? Pick out the words that suggest her attitude.

5. Pick out the descriptions and images she uses to describe her husband (in stanza one) and the teenage boys (in stanza two). Annotate these descriptions/images in as much detail as you can, and think about how her views of love and relationships have changed now that she is older.

6. Rita Dove addresses her husband directly as 'you' in the poem. What effect do you think this has on the reader?

AO2 Looking more closely at structure and form

ACTIVITY 3

1. Each stanza focuses on a different aspect of the relationship. What does Dove tell the reader about her feelings in each stanza? Refer closely to the words of the poem.

2. What do you think is the effect of the enjambment between stanzas two and three?

3. The rhyme pattern in the first two stanzas is quite lyrical and creates a sing-song effect. In the final stanza, the rhyme pattern and lyrical feeling is not as obvious. What effect do you think the poet was hoping to achieve by doing this?

Thinking about themes

ACTIVITY 4

1. Look at the first stanza. Pick out the words that suggest the closeness of the poet's relationship with her husband.

2. What do you think the following lines suggest about their relationship?

> Still, it's embarrassing, this happiness –
> Who's satisfied simply with what's good for us,
> When has the ordinary ever been news?

3. The title 'Cozy Apologia' literally means 'a comfortable apology'. What do you think the poet is apologising for? Do you think her tone is genuine or sarcastic? Find evidence to prove your ideas.

 Developing your own individual response

 **ACTIVITY 5**

(1) Which adjective best describes the mood of the poem? Find evidence from the poem to back up your ideas.

romantic	sarcastic	melancholic	sentimental
challenging	argumentative	warm	something else?

(2) Throughout the poem, Dove uses parenthesis. Find examples of where she does this and decide what effect this technique creates.

(3) Try to explain what you understand by the line, 'We're content, but fall short of the Divine'.

 TIP

You will achieve a higher mark if you make detailed reference to the language a poet uses.

Self-assessment

ACTIVITY 6

Answer true or false to the following statements.

I can comment on and find evidence for how:

- Dove presents the relationship between her husband and herself
- Dove uses language to create effects
- the poem relates to the context in which it was written.

If you answered 'false' to any of the statements, read the poem again and use your answers to the questions on these pages to help you.

Working on exam skills

 ACTIVITY 7

Look at this example of an exam-style question.

> How does Dove write about relationships in this poem?

Write a section on language and imagery that you could include in your answer.

Remember to:

- Make a clear point.
- Use evidence from the poem to support your point.
- Explain the effect of the evidence/quotations you have used.
- Focus on particular word choices.

 ACTIVITY 8

Now read the following paragraph written by a student.

In this poem, Rita Dove wants to emphasise how 'cozy' and comfortable she feels with her choice of partner despite the disapproval of society. She is totally absorbed by her husband as everything she looks at reminds her of him, from the power of the natural elements, 'the wind-still rain', to the mundane and ordinary 'glossy blue' ink of her pen. Perhaps this suggests she also views him as some sort of muse-like inspiration figure to help her explore her creative feelings. She goes on to associate him with being a 'hero'-like figure. This makes us think that he is a powerful, reliable and protective force for her.

Find examples of where:

- this paragraph begins with a clear point
- the student uses evidence from the poem
- the student explains the effect of the quotations used
- the student focuses on particular word choices.

Compare with...

'Cozy Apologia' could be compared with: 'Sonnet 43'; 'Valentine'; 'She Walks in Beauty'; 'Afternoons'; 'The Manhunt'.

 ACTIVITY 9

After reading the sample answer, if you think you need to add anything to your paragraphs from Activity 7, redraft them now.

'Valentine' by Carol Ann Duffy

OBJECTIVES

▶ To explore and develop your response to 'Valentine' by Carol Ann Duffy.
▶ To understand how Duffy uses language, structure and form to present relationships.
▶ To understand some of the contexts of the poem.

Introduction

In this poem, Carol Ann Duffy describes an unusual Valentine's Day gift – an onion!

AO3 Context

Carol Ann Duffy was born in 1955 and she is the UK's first female Poet Laureate. In this poem she chooses to criticise the conventional and clichéd symbols of romance and relationships.

AO1 First thoughts

ACTIVITY 1

1. Make a list of the all the traditional symbols or images of love that you can think of. You can also use the images that Duffy mentions in the poem.
2. Think of three questions you have about the lines below, and write them down. Explain why you want these questions to be answered.

> I give you an onion.
> It is a moon wrapped in brown paper.

3. Duffy writes that an onion 'will blind you with tears/like a lover'. How can an onion blind you with tears? How can a lover blind you with tears?

Glossary

kissogram – someone who dresses up as a character, goes to parties and kisses people

platinum – a valuable metal, often used for wedding rings

lethal – deadly/fatal

AO2 Looking more closely at words and images

ACTIVITY 2

1. Duffy introduces the onion as a symbol of love and she compares it to 'a moon wrapped in brown paper'. What connections can you make between the following images that Duffy creates? Annotate each of these images to express your thoughts:

   An onion   the moon   brown paper   undressing   love

2. Duffy uses a range of images to build up a picture in the reader's mind. Explore some of these by copying and completing the following table. You can add any other points or quotes you think are relevant.

Point made in the poem	Quote	Effect of the language
The positive side of love shown by the hope and optimism at the start of a relationship.	it promises light/like the careful undressing of love	
Love can be harsh and hurtful.		
	Its fierce kiss will stay/on your lips	
		The smallest, innermost part of an onion is described as looking like a wedding ring.
	Possessive and faithful/as we are for as long as we are	

3. At the start of two stanzas, Duffy uses commanding, blunt language: 'Here.' 'Take it.' What do these lines suggest about what Duffy is doing? How do you think her lover has been reacting to what she has been saying?

4. How can an onion 'make your reflection a wobbling photo of grief'?

5. Find two examples of alliteration in the poem. What do you think Duffy is suggesting about the overuse of alliteration in love poems?

AO2 Looking more closely at structure and form

 **ACTIVITY 3**

(1) Some people think that the poem follows the journey of a relationship from the beginning to the end. Can you find evidence in the poem to support this view?

(2) The poem is written in free verse and each stanza is very short, with some being only one line long. What effect do the short stanzas have?

(3) Why do you think 'Lethal.' is given a line to itself?

Thinking about themes

 **ACTIVITY 4**

(1) How would you describe Duffy's attitude to love? You might want to consider some of the following adjectives:

    romantic   sentimental realistic   challenging

    stereotypical   traditional   clichéd   obsessive   cynical

(2) Is her attitude positive or negative, or both? Find evidence from the poem to back up your opinion.

(3) Do you think Duffy expects love to be everlasting? Explain your opinion by referring to words from the poem.

 Developing your own individual response

 ACTIVITY 5

(1) The ending of the poem is sometimes thought to be quite threatening and unsettling. What is your reaction to the ending of the poem?

(2) Why do you think the 'platinum loops shrink' at the end? What do you think this implies about a relationship?

(3) Has the poem changed the way in which you think about love? Explain why or why not. Remember to refer to the poem in your answer.

(4) Think of four words to describe the effect this poem had on you.

 TIP

Try to talk about the structure of the poem but always support this with detail.

Self-assessment

 ACTIVITY 6

Answer true or false to the following statements.

I can comment on and find evidence for how Duffy:

- uses language to communicate her attitude to love
- uses imagery to portray different aspects of love.

If you answered 'false' to either of the statements, read the poem again and use your answers to the questions on these pages to help you.

Working on exam skills

 ACTIVITY 7

Look at these examples of exam-style questions.

> Write about how Duffy presents the complicated nature of relationships in 'Valentine'.

Write a section on language and imagery that you could include in your answers.

Remember to:

- Make a clear point.
- Use evidence from the poem to support your point.
- Explain the effect of the evidence/quotations you have used.
- Focus on particular word choices.

 ACTIVITY 8

Now read the following paragraph written by a student.

Duffy seems to be both realistic and a bit cynical about relationships in this poem. She doesn't want to be restricted by traditional and clichéd images of love like 'cute cards' and 'satin hearts', but instead she wants to give a more practical and useful gift like an 'onion' because she thinks it says more about the true nature of love. Duffy uses negative language from the very beginning by using the word 'not' and there are several negative words in the rest of the poem. For example, she describes love as 'possessive', which suggests love can make a person obsessive, a trait that could ultimately destroy any relationship.

Find examples of where:

- this paragraph begins with a clear point
- the student uses evidence from the poem
- the student explains the effect of the quotations used
- the student focuses on particular word choices.

ACTIVITY 9

After reading the sample answer, if you think you need to add anything to your paragraphs from Activity 7, redraft them now.

Look at the Assessment Objectives on p. 5.

- Which criteria do you think you have shown in your answer?
- What do you think you need to do to improve your performance?

Compare with...

'Valentine' could be compared with: 'The Manhunt'; 'Sonnet 43'; 'She Walks in Beauty'; 'Cozy Apologia'; 'A Wife in London'; 'Afternoons'.

'A Wife in London' by Thomas Hardy

OBJECTIVES

▶ To explore and develop your response to 'A Wife in London' by Thomas Hardy.

▶ To understand how Hardy uses language, structure and form to evoke sympathy in the reader.

▶ To understand some of the contexts of the poem.

Introduction

The poem is about a wife waiting for news about her husband, who is fighting in the Boer War in South Africa.

Thomas Hardy (1840–1928) was an English poet and novelist who often focused on tragedy in his writing.

AO3 Context

Hardy wrote the poem in 1899. In the poem he is referring to the Boer War, which was fought in South Africa between 1880 and 1881. The Boers were farmers who rebelled against British rule in the Transvaal in northern South Africa in a bid to re-establish their independence.

The references to the thick fog tell us about the thick London smog that was common in the late nineteenth and early twentieth centuries. This fog was the result of smoke and mists coming in from the sea. This mixture of fog and smoke was called 'smog' or a 'pea souper'.

Glossary

tawny vapour – brown fog

webby fold on fold – the fog was like a spider's web

waning – going out

taper – thin candle used to light fires/lamps

jaunts – trips

brake and burn – woods and stream

morrow – the next day

AO1 First thoughts

ACTIVITY 1

(1) Summarise briefly what happens in each stanza.

(2) Write a list of the words that you think have negative connotations. Then write a list of the more positive words. Which list is longer? What do you think this suggests about the atmosphere of the poem?

AO2 Looking more closely at words and images

📄 ACTIVITY 2

1 In the first stanza, Hardy creates a very gloomy and ominous atmosphere. Look at the quotations below. Copy and complete the grid, noting the poet's techniques and the effect on the reader.

Quote	Technique	Effect on the reader
Tawny vapour	Pathetic fallacy	Creates picture of dark, miserable London
Webby fold on fold		
Like a waning taper		
street lamp glimmers cold		

2 Can you pick out words and phrases from the first stanza that create a feeling of claustrophobia and entrapment? Why do you think Hardy wanted to create this feeling?

3 Hardy wrote the poem in the present tense. Find examples from the poem to prove this and think about why he chose to write in the present tense and not the past tense.

4 In the first verse, 'sits' is a very passive verb. What do you think Hardy's intention was in using this word?

5 Hardy uses the euphemism 'fallen' to tell us of the soldier's death. Why do you think he does this?

6 Why do you think the subheading of the second part of the poem is 'The Irony'? What do you find ironic about these stanzas?

AO2 Looking more closely at structure and form

📄 ACTIVITY 3

1 The pace of the poem changes at the start of the second stanza. Find words that suggest this change. What technique does the poet use to suggest this change?

2 The line 'Of meaning it dazes to understand' sounds quite awkward. Why do you think Hardy has deliberately constructed the line in such a way?

③ What do you notice about the punctuation in the line, 'He – has fallen – in the far South Land…'? What effect do you think Hardy was trying to achieve here?

④ The poem has a regular ABBAB rhyme pattern yet it doesn't have a 'sing-song' quality. What effect does this create, and how does this affect the mood of the poem?

Thinking about themes

📄 ACTIVITY 4

① How does Hardy stress the sense of lost potential in the final verse? Do you think the poet approved of warfare?

② Do you consider 'A Wife in London' to be primarily a poem about war, grief or relationships? Refer closely to evidence from the poem.

AO1 Developing your own individual response

📄 ACTIVITY 5

① How effective is the poem's title, 'A Wife in London'? Support your opinion with evidence from the poem.

(2) Hardy uses the weather to highlight the feelings of the characters.
Below is one student's mind map about this technique and its uses.
Study the ideas and add at least three of your own.

'The street-lamp glimmers cold' suggests the lights are flickering and fading. This could be symbolic of the life of the soldier, which is also flickering out.

'In the summer weather' suggests the hope and optimism the soldier feels when writing the letter.

Hardy's use of the weather

It is sadly ironic that he has died before his wife reads the message.

The picture created is bright and cheerful and 'new love' suggests he sees a new beginning for them.

(3) Which line or lines in the poem had the greatest effect on you? Explain your choice by referring to the poem.

(4) Which do you think is the most hard-hitting line in the poem? Explain your choice.

! TIP

Practise evaluating the ways in which a poet expresses his/her ideas and achieves effects.

Self-assessment

 **ACTIVITY 6**

Answer true or false to the following statements.

I can comment on and find evidence for how:

- Hardy uses language to communicate his feelings about loss
- Hardy uses structure and form to present his ideas
- Hardy uses pathetic fallacy to create atmosphere
- the poem relates to the context in which it was written.

If you answered 'false' to any of the statements, read the poem again and use your answers to the questions on these pages to help you.

Working on exam skills

 ACTIVITY 7

Look at the following range of different responses to this exam-style question.

> How does Hardy write about the effects of war in the poem 'A Wife in London'?

Student A

The poet creates a melancholy and depressing atmosphere.

Student B

The poet doesn't really focus on the manner of the soldier's death but instead concentrates of the loss felt by his wife at home.

Student C

The poet shows how the love that the young couple once had, is now wasted.

Turn each of these responses into Point–Evidence–Explain paragraphs by:
- finding words and evidence from the poem for each response
- writing a few sentences about how the poet uses language and its effects.

 ACTIVITY 8

Now annotate your paragraphs to show where you have:
- made a clear point
- used evidence from the poem
- explained the effect of the quotations used
- focused on particular word choices.

 ACTIVITY 9

Now look at the Assessment Objectives on p. 5.
- Which criteria do you think you have shown in your answer?
- What do you think you need to do to improve your performance?

> **Compare with…**
> 'A Wife in London' could be compared with: 'The Manhunt'; 'The Soldier'; 'Dulce et Decorum Est'; 'Mametz Wood'.

'Death of a Naturalist' by Seamus Heaney

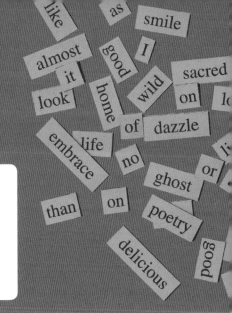

OBJECTIVES

▶ To explore and develop your response to 'Death of a Naturalist' by Seamus Heaney.

▶ To understand how Heaney uses language, structure and form to suggest the loss of innocence.

▶ To understand some of the contexts of the poem.

Introduction

This poem describes the memories of a young boy who has been collecting frogspawn from a flax dam.

AO3 Context

Seamus Heaney (1939–2013) was an Irish poet who wrote poems about Ireland, rural life and nature. He won the Nobel Prize for Literature in 1995.

AO1 First thoughts

ACTIVITY 1

1. What are your initial thoughts about the poem's title, 'Death of a Naturalist'? What do you think the poem is going to be about?

2. Summarise in two sentences what happens in the first stanza. Summarise in one sentence what happens in the second stanza.

3. Read lines 1–7. Underline any positive words/images. Circle any negative words/images.

Glossary

naturalist – an expert in nature and the natural world

flax-dam – a pool where bundles of flax (a plant) are placed to soften the stems from which linen is made

festered – decayed/rotted

townland – a small territorial division of land in Ireland

sods – clumps of earth or mud

gauze – a thin transparent fabric

rank – foul-smelling

vengeance – revenge

AO2 Looking more closely at words and images

ACTIVITY 2

1. At what time of year is the poem set? Find evidence from the poem to support your opinion. Why do you think Heaney chose this particular time of year?

2. Look at the first stanza again. Find words to show that the narrator is feeling excited and enthusiastic.

3. How old do you think the child is? Find evidence from the poem to back up your ideas.

4. Choose four of the following quotes and annotate them in detail to explain your thoughts about what the words/images suggest.

   the flax dam festered

   Bubbles gargled delicately

   bluebottles / Wove a strong gauze of sound around the smell

   the warm thick slobber / Of frogspawn that grew like clotted water

   The fattening dots burst, into nimble / Swimming tadpoles

5. The mood of the second stanza is very different. Look at how each combination of words listed below is used, and write a sentence or two about why you think Heaney chooses each one (an example is given for you).

rank	gross bellied frogs
the angry frogs / Invaded	Poised like mud grenades
coarse croaking	The great slime kings

Example

Describing the fields as 'rank' suggests the child's senses are being attacked or assaulted by something rotten and foul-smelling. It seems an overpowering stench.

AO2 Looking more closely at structure and form

📄 ACTIVITY 3

1. The poem is clearly divided into two very distinct sections with contrasting moods. Why do you think the child's feelings have changed by the end of the poem?

2. Heaney uses the technique of onomatopoeia to bring this scene to life. What examples of onomatopoeia can you find in lines 27–30? Write them down and explain the effects created.

3. The atmosphere of the second stanza is more threatening. Try to explain how this atmosphere is created by some of the words and the sounds used in lines 22–25 and lines 26–33.

4. Look at lines 7–10. What do the punctuation and rhythm in these lines suggest about the child's feelings?

Thinking about themes

 ACTIVITY 4

1. The poet suggests how childlike innocence can be lost as the child begins to realise that the world can be a complex and sometimes uncomfortable place. Draw a mind map to chart the child's gradual loss of innocence, with quotes to back up your points.

2. The poem also deals with the theme of change or transformation. How many examples of transformation can you find in the poem? Write down as many as you can find and think about how the poet suggests this transformation. For example, 'spring' becomes 'one hot day'; 'mammy' and 'daddy frog' become 'angry' 'kings'.

 Developing your own individual response

 ACTIVITY 5

1. What, in your opinion, is the most vivid and memorable description of nature in the poem? Explain your choice.

2. No one actually dies in the poem. What do you think the poet was suggesting by using the title 'Death of a Naturalist'? Think of and write down two or three other suitable titles for the poem. Explain your choices.

3. What have you learned about the process of growing up after reading the poem?

> **! TIP**
>
> You will get credit for your ideas as long as they are backed up by evidence from the poem. It is a sensible idea to use vocabulary such as 'perhaps' and 'maybe' to show that you realise there may be more than one possible interpretation.

Self-assessment

 ACTIVITY 6

Answer true or false to the following statements.

I can comment on and find evidence for how Heaney:

- presents the theme of growing up and losing one's innocence
- uses language to show the child's changing feelings
- uses techniques to create vivid and evocative images.

If you answered 'false' to any of the statements, read the poem again and use your answers to the questions on these pages to help you.

Working on exam skills

 ACTIVITY 7

Look at the following range of different responses to this exam-style question:

> How does Heaney present nature in the poem 'Death of a Naturalist'?

Student A

In the first stanza the poet emphasises how peaceful, idyllic and welcoming nature can be.

Student B

The poet uses the technique of onomatopoeia to suggest the sense of horror and fear experienced by the child.

Student C

The comfortable childhood routine soon becomes a nightmarish encounter.

Turn each of these responses into Point–Evidence–Explain paragraphs by:
- finding words and evidence from the poem for each response
- writing a few sentences about how the poet uses language and its effects.

 ACTIVITY 8

Now annotate your paragraphs to show where you have:
- made a clear point
- used evidence from the poem
- explained the effect of the quotations used
- focused on particular word choices.

 ACTIVITY 9

Now look at the Assessment Objectives on p. 5.
- Which criteria do you think you have shown in your answer?
- What do you think you need to do to improve your performance?

Compare with…
'Death of a Naturalist' could be compared with: 'To Autumn'; 'The Prelude'; 'Living Space'; 'As Imperceptibly as Grief'; 'Afternoons'.

'Hawk Roosting' by Ted Hughes

OBJECTIVES

▶ To explore and develop your response to 'Hawk Roosting' by Ted Hughes.
▶ To understand how the poet uses language to present the theme of power.
▶ To understand how the poet creates a threatening picture of nature.

Introduction

This poem is written from the point of view of a hawk as he sits at the top of a wood.

AO3 Context

Ted Hughes (1939–98) was born in Yorkshire. He was a well-known poet and he married an American poet, Sylvia Plath. He was the Poet Laureate from 1984 until his death in 1998. 'Hawk Roosting' is from a collection of poems about animals and nature called *Lupercal*, published in 1960. When this poem was first published, it was quite controversial. The image of the hawk sitting on top of the world controlling everything with the threat of violence made people think of a Fascist dictator – the symbol of Nazism was an eagle standing on top of a wreath.

AO1 First thoughts

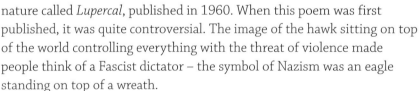

ACTIVITY 1

① A hawk is a bird of prey. Write down any ideas you can think of connected with a hawk, its behaviour and how it is often presented in literature and history.

② What two questions would you like to ask the hawk?

③ The poem is written in the first person and as a dramatic monologue. How do you think a reader would respond to this?

Glossary

hawk – a bird of prey
falsifying – deceptively/deliberately untrue
buoyancy – supportiveness
sophistry – false but clever argument
allotment – dealing out/allocation
assert – declare/argue

AO2 Looking more closely at words and image

ACTIVITY 2

(1) How many times is the word 'I' used in the poem? What do you think this suggests about the hawk's attitude?

(2) Here are some adjectives which could be used to describe the hawk. Read the list carefully; which ones create a positive image of the hawk, and which ones create a more negative impression?

calm   proud   calculating   thoughtful   skilful
peaceful   dignified   omnipotent   aggressive
self-assured   confident   intelligent   determined

Students should add any further positive or negative adjectives they can think of.

(3) Pick out two positive adjectives and two negative ones from the above list. Find a quote from the poem to support each one and write a sentence or two about each.

(4) Hughes uses many techniques to create this picture of the hawk. Complete the table below, listing the techniques that have been used and adding some of your own. Find an example of each technique in the poem and discuss the effect that is created.

Technique	Quote	Effect created
Personification	My feet are locked	Stresses the link between the hawk and humans
Repetition		
Violent words		
Use of exclamation mark		
Symbolism		
Very short sentences		

AO2 ## Looking more closely at structure and form

 ACTIVITY 3

1. The poem is written in an organised way so that each stanza focuses on a different aspect of the hawk. Draw a storyboard to illustrate the focus of each stanza, and pick out one quote to represent each stanza.

2. The structure of the poem could be described as circular, as both the first line and the last line begin with the word 'I'. Why do you think the poet has used this structure?

3. In the first stanza the long 'ee' sound is used four times. Pick out the examples and explain what effect the poet is trying to create here.

4. In the last stanza, there is one fairly short line and four statements. What effect do you think the poet was trying to achieve by doing this?

Thinking about themes

ACTIVITY 4

1. Some people have suggested that the hawk could be related to the theme of power and ambition. Look for some words and images in the poem that could support this idea.

2. In what ways do you think the poem could be related to human society? If you think the poem could be referring to a person, what type of person would it be? Find evidence from the poem to support your ideas.

 AO1 ## Developing your own individual response

ACTIVITY 5

1. In stanza three, why do you think the poet has capitalised the word 'Creation'?

2. Do you think the fact that the hawk sits 'in the top of the wood' could be interpreted literally and metaphorically? Try to explain the literal and metaphorical meaning of the phrase.

3 Read these four viewpoints on the poem. Decide which opinion you agree with most strongly, and explain your ideas by referring to the words in the poem.

Student A

The poet is praising the single-mindedness, determination and power of the hawk.

Student B

The poet has a neutral attitude to the hawk because he describes it quite objectively.

Student C

The poet is using the hawk as a metaphor to show the extreme state of mind of a human killer or a dictator.

Student D

The poet is simply describing a darker and more brutal side of nature.

4 Has this poem changed the way you think about nature and the natural world? Explain why or why not by referring to the poem.

Self-assessment

 ACTIVITY 6

Answer true or false to the following statements.

I can comment on and find evidence for how Hughes:

- uses language to describe the hawk
- explores the themes of power and ambition
- uses structure and form to create effects.

If you answered 'false' to any of the statements, read the poem again and use your answers to the questions on these pages to help you.

! TIP

When you write about a poem, try to decide what the mood of the poem is and how it has been created.

Working on exam skills

 TIP

The tone of a poem is the attitude that the style implies. You can work out the tone of a poem by the language and syntax used by the poet.

The mood is the atmosphere of a poem created through language and setting, etc.

Mood and tone evoke certain feelings and emotions in the reader.

 ACTIVITY 7

Look at this exam-style question.

> How does Ted Hughes present the violent and aggressive side of nature in 'Hawk Roosting'?

- Write a section on language and tone that you could include in your answer.
- Write a section on form and structure that you could include in your answer.

 ACTIVITY 8

Now read the following paragraph written by a student.

> Hughes presents the violent and aggressive side of nature by creating a dramatic monologue from the point of view of a hawk — a bird of prey. The hawk is described as being merciless and fearlessly aggressive because 'I kill where I please', suggesting he enjoys the thought and act of killing. The brutality of 'tearing off heads' emphasises the ruthlessness and power of the hawk, but at the same time we see that he can be calm and collected about what he does from the more restrained language of the second stanza: 'convenience', 'buoyancy', 'advantage' and 'inspection'. Perhaps Hughes is suggesting how the hawk, a killing machine, is able to distance himself from what he does.

Find examples of where:

- this paragraph begins with a clear point
- the student uses evidence from the poem
- the student explains the effect of the quotations used
- the student focuses on particular word choices.

 ACTIVITY 9

Redraft your paragraphs from Activity 7 if you think you need to add anything to them.

Now look at the Assessment Objectives on p. 5.

- Which criteria do you think you have shown in your answer?
- What do you think you need to do to improve your performance?

Compare with...
'Hawk Roosting' could be compared with: 'The Prelude'; 'To Autumn'; 'Death of a Naturalist'; 'Ozymandias'.

'To Autumn' by John Keats

OBJECTIVES

▶ To explore and develop your response to 'To Autumn' by John Keats.
▶ To understand how Keats uses language, structure and form to describe the seasons.
▶ To understand some of the contexts of the poem.

Introduction

In this poem, Keats describes the richness and wonders of the season of autumn.

AO3 Context

John Keats (1795–1821) was a Romantic poet (along with Blake, Wordsworth, Coleridge, Byron and Shelley). 'To Autumn' was written in 1819 on an autumn evening after Keats returned from a walk near Winchester. It is the final poem in a sequence of odes Keats wrote in 1819. An 'ode' is a poem usually addressed to an inanimate object or abstract idea that cannot respond.

In the poem, Keats compares autumn to a female goddess. At the time, the seasons were often depicted as women in European art.

AO1 First thoughts

ACTIVITY 1

1. Create a word bank for autumn. Write down a list of words to describe the sights, sounds, atmosphere and mood connected with autumn. Try to cover the five senses (taste, touch, smell, sound, sight). Do any of your ideas match up with images created by Keats? If so, match them up.

2. Many of the words in the poem are quite old-fashioned or archaic. Pick out three words that are not used today and try to work out what their modern equivalent would be.

> **Glossary**
>
> **gourd** – a large fruit
> **kernel** – the edible part of a nut
> **o'er-brimm'd** – over-filled
> **thee** – you
> **thy** – your
> **gleaner** – a person who gathered up the scraps left after the harvest
> **bourn** – small stream

AO2 Looking more closely at words and images

ACTIVITY 2

1. Find three examples in the first stanza to suggest that autumn is a season of calm and contentment.

2. Keats personifies autumn in the poem. Find examples of where Keats uses this technique in each stanza. Write out the quotes and annotate them in as much detail as you can.

3. Keats uses many adjectives in the poem (in fact there are very few nouns without an adjective!). Select five of your favourite adjectives and explain what you think they add to the poem.

4. Autumn is described as the season of harvest and abundance, and the richness of the language used by Keats supports this. Find examples of this in the poem; for instance, the vines are 'loaded' with fruit.

5. Find and write down examples of rhetorical questions in the poem. What do you notice about the different tone of each question?

AO2 Looking more closely at structure and form

 ACTIVITY 3

1. It has been suggested there are three separate stages to this poem. What do you think the stages might be? Find a quote to back up your opinion.

2. The poem is written in iambic pentameter in three stanzas of 11 lines each. What do you notice about the first four lines of each stanza? What do you notice about the last seven lines of each stanza?

Thinking about themes

 ACTIVITY 4

1. The poem has been described as a 'pastoral' poem because it is inspired by life in a rural setting. What traditional images of the pleasures of the English countryside can you find? Write the images down and annotate them.

2. The theme of the passing of time is suggested in the poem. Find evidence for this in the poem.

3. In the final stanza Keats uses some words and images connected with death. Write down these words and think about how they might change the tone and atmosphere of the stanza. What do you think Keats is suggesting about life and death? In what way do you think this poem suggests Keats' awareness of his own mortality?

AO1 Developing your own individual response

 ACTIVITY 5

1. Look at the two opinions about the poem expressed over the page. They are both valid, but which one do you agree with the most? Support your ideas by referring to words and phrases from the poem.

Student A

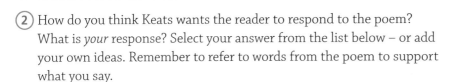

The poem is really moving because Keats is aware of how quickly time passes and he wants to show the reader that he has accepted this and the inevitability of death.

Student B

I think the poem is simply describing the richness and fecundity of nature.

(2) How do you think Keats wants the reader to respond to the poem? What is *your* response? Select your answer from the list below – or add your own ideas. Remember to refer to words from the poem to support what you say.

awe   admiration   loss   disappointment
fear   inevitability   regret   pain

> **! TIP**
>
> Always try to give a clear overview of the whole poem before you begin to discuss aspects of form and language in more detail. This will show the examiner that you really understand the poem.

Self-assessment

ACTIVITY 6

Answer true or false to the following statements.

I can comment on and find evidence for how Keats:

- uses language to present autumn
- uses structure and form to write about the passing of time.

If you answered 'false' to either of the statements, read the poem again and use your answers to the questions on these pages to help you.

Working on exam skills

 ACTIVITY 7

Look at this example of an exam-style question.

> Write about the ways in which Keats presents nature in this poem.

Choose three of the quotations listed below and use them to write three paragraphs in which you:
- respond to the text
- comment on the way the poet has used language, structure and form to create meaning and effect
- show you understand the contexts in which the poem was written.

> Season of mists and mellow fruitfulness,
> Close bosom friend of the maturing sun.
>
> Sometimes whoever seeks abroad may find
> Thee sitting careless on a granary floor,
> Thy hair soft-lifted by the winnowing wind
>
> Where are the songs of Spring? Aye, where are they?
> Think not of them, thou hast thy music too, –
>
> While barred clouds bloom the soft-dying day,
> And touch the stubble plains with rosy hue
>   and now with treble soft
> The red-breast whistles from a garden-croft;
> And gathering swallows twitter in the skies.

 ACTIVITY 8

Now annotate your answer to show where you have:
- made a clear point to start a paragraph
- used evidence from the poem
- explained the effect of the quotation used
- focused on particular word choices.

ACTIVITY 9

Now look at the Assessment Objectives on p. 5.

- Which criteria do you think you have shown in your answer?
- What do you think you need to do to improve your performance?

Compare with…

'To Autumn' could be compared with: 'The Prelude'; 'As Imperceptibly as Grief'; 'Death of a Naturalist'; 'Afternoons'.

'Afternoons' by Philip Larkin

OBJECTIVES

▶ To explore and develop your response to 'Afternoons' by Philip Larkin.
▶ To understand how Larkin uses language, structure and form to write about the passing of time.
▶ To understand some of the contexts of the poem.

Introduction

In this poem Larkin is describing young mothers watching their children as they play on the swings.

AO3 Context

Philip Larkin (1922–85) was an English poet famous for creating detailed observations about everyday life and relationships. People often thought his poetry was rather negative and miserable. His life was quite restricted as he never married, had no children, never travelled abroad and worked as a librarian in Hull for 30 years.

AO1 First thoughts

 ACTIVITY 1

① Summarise what happens in the poem in two short sentences.
② The poem is describing the lives of young mothers who have had to grow up quickly and take on responsibilities. Imagine a time in the future when you are in your mid-twenties. What do you think your life will be like then? How would you like your life to be?
Are there any words or phrases in the poem that are unappealing about growing up?

> **Glossary**
>
> **recreation ground** – playground
> **skilled trades** – manual jobs that need a certain set of skills, such as plumbers, carpenters, electricians
> **courting places** – areas where lovers meet

AO2 Looking more closely at words and images

📄 ACTIVITY 2

(1) Look at the words below and pick out the ones that seem most appropriate to describe the mood of the poem. Then find and write down a quote from the poem to support each choice.

bored	busy	miserable	relaxed	nervous
calm	stressed	positive	hopeful	energetic
disillusioned	negative	melancholic	romantic	
neglected	vibrant	frustrated	unfulfilled	

(2) Why do you think the poet has chosen the word 'assemble' instead of 'meet' in the first verse? What do you think this suggests about the type of lives the women lead?

(3) What do you learn about the relationships the women have with their husbands in the second verse? Have these relationships changed over the course of time? Refer to the words in the poem to support your ideas.

(4) Read these lines from the poem carefully and annotate them to explain your thoughts and feelings about them. An example is given below.

Summer is fading: ←———— The seasons are gradually changing so time is moving on.

At swing and sandpit

Setting free their children. ← The women are growing older and losing their youth; summer is often associated with youth; are they now feeling older than their actual age because of all their responsibilities?

(But the lovers are all in school) ← Fading is a gradual, not a sudden, movement so perhaps, like time, their lives are slipping away from them without them really noticing how it is happening.

Their beauty has thickened. ↙

Their beauty is also fading because of their stress, frustration and lack of fulfilment.

 Looking more closely at structure and form

ACTIVITY 3

(1) The poem is written in three stanzas of equal length, and each stanza has a different focus. If you were asked to draw a symbol to represent the main idea in each stanza, what would you draw? Explain your choice.

(2) The poet uses the technique of enjambment in this poem. Write down three examples of this technique from the poem and explain what effect you think the poet wanted to create.

(3) In the poem, there are no exclamations or dramatically short lines, only statements. Why do you think the poet has chosen to write in this way?

Thinking about themes

 ## ACTIVITY 4

(1) Larkin writes about restriction and entrapment in this poem. Do you agree or disagree with this viewpoint? Explain your answer by referring to words in the poem.

(2) Some people feel this is quite a sad poem because the poet creates so many images of things fading and ending. Do you agree or disagree with this viewpoint? Write down the words/images that are connected with things coming to an end and those which suggest things are developing and growing.

(3) Time and its passing are important in the poem. How do you think the poet shows a contrast between the mothers and their children? Refer to words in the poem to support your explanation.

AO1 Developing your own individual response

 ACTIVITY 5

(1) Why do you think Larkin chose 'Afternoons' as the title for the poem? Do you think there could be a literal and a metaphorical meaning?

(2) What do you understand by the final two lines of the poem? How do you respond to this ending:

> Something is pushing them
> To the side of their own lives.

 TIP

Remember to include your own personal response when writing about a poem.

(3) Do you feel sympathetic towards the women in the poem? Refer to the words in the poem to explain your answer.

(4) Do you feel optimistic or pessimistic about the future after reading this poem? Explain your response by referring to words from the poem.

Self-assessment

ACTIVITY 6

Answer true or false to the following statements.

I can comment on and find evidence for how Larkin:

- presents the theme of time passing
- uses language to present the relationships between the husbands and wives
- uses techniques to create meaning and effect.

If you answered 'false' to any of the statements, read the poem again and use your answers to the questions on these pages to help you.

Working on exam skills

 ACTIVITY 7

Look at this example of an exam-style question.

> How does Larkin write about male/female relationships in 'Afternoons'?

Choose three of the quotations below and use them to write three short paragraphs in which you:

- respond to the task by giving your own individual thoughts
- look closely at the language, words and images used.

> In the hollows of afternoons
> Young mothers assemble
>
> Behind them, at intervals,
> Stand husbands in skilled trades
>
> And the albums, lettered
> Our Wedding, lying
> Near the television:
>
> Before them, the wind
> Is ruining their courting-places
>
> Something is pushing them
> To the side of their own lives

 ACTIVITY 8

Annotate your paragraphs to show where you have:

- made a clear point
- used evidence from the poem
- explained the effect of the quotations used
- focused on particular word choices.

 ACTIVITY 9

Now look at the Assessment Objectives on p. 5.

- Which criteria do you think you have shown in your answer?
- What do you think you need to do to improve your performance?

Compare with…

'Afternoons' could be compared with: 'The Manhunt'; 'Sonnet 43'; 'Valentine'; 'To Autumn'; 'As Imperceptibly as Grief'; 'Cozy Apologia'.

'Dulce et Decorum Est' by Wilfred Owen

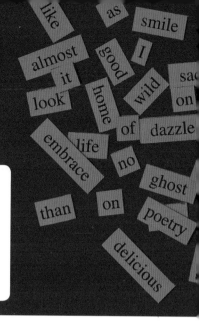

OBJECTIVES

▶ To explore and develop your response to 'Dulce et Decorum Est' by Wilfred Owen.

▶ To understand how Wilfred Owen has used language, structure and form to express his feelings about war and death.

▶ To understand some of the contexts of the poem.

Introduction

In this poem Wilfred Owen describes a gas attack in the trenches during World War I (1914–18).

AO3 Context

Wilfred Owen (1893–1918) fought in World War I. In 1914, at the start of the war, people were very naïve and excited about the thought of fighting the Germans. The war was expected to be over by Christmas but instead it lasted for four years. As a result of this, propaganda was needed to recruit soldiers, and Jessie Pope wrote the poem 'Who's For the Game?' to encourage young men to enlist by comparing warfare to a game. Wilfred Owen wrote 'Dulce et Decorum Est' in response because he wanted to show the brutality and horrors of war. The Latin title of the poem is taken from the Roman poet Horace, and Owen has used it ironically. Owen died in 1918, two days before the end of the war, and his poem was published posthumously.

Glossary

hags – witch-like old women

fatigue – exhaustion

ecstasy – frenzy

flound'ring – staggering

lime – a chemical that can burn the skin

ardent – desperate/ intensely enthusiastic

dulce et decorum est pro patria mori – it is a sweet and honourable thing to die for your country

ACTIVITY 1

AO1 First thoughts

1. How would you describe the stereotypical image of a soldier?
2. Each stanza describes something different. What happens in each stanza?
3. What is your reaction to the opening two lines of the poem?
4. If you could ask Wilfred Owen two questions about the poem, what would they be?

AO2 Looking more closely at words and images

📄 ACTIVITY 2

① Read the first stanza carefully and underline all the words and phrases that describe the soldiers. Do you think these words create positive or negative images of the soldiers and the conditions? Annotate the words you have selected in as much detail as you can. Here is an example to help you.

They are hunched and bent over to try to protect themselves? Suggests they have lost the pride and dignity they had at the start of the war?

'sacks' could suggest how ragged and torn their uniforms have become?

Bent double, like old beggars under sacks

The soldiers have aged prematurely, perhaps because of the horrific conditions? Perhaps because of the horrors they have seen? Suggests they are suffering physically and emotionally?

'beggers' suggests that they have lost their pride and self-respect? Suggests their loss of humanity/ they have been stripped of their humanity? Suggests they feel worthless, degraded and neglected?

② Think of three adjectives to describe the mood and atmosphere of the first stanza. Find evidence from the stanza to support each idea.

③ How does the poet make the gas attack sound terrifying in the second stanza? Pick out words and phrases to support your ideas.

④ Look at the final stanza again. Write down all the words Owen has used to describe the dying soldier. What effect do you think Owen wanted these words to have on the reader?

⑤ Owen uses a range of techniques to build up a picture of this horrifying experience in the reader's mind. Explore how these techniques work by copying and completing the following table. You can add any other points you think are relevant.

Technique	Quote	Effect
Simile		
First person narrator		
Onomatopoeia		
Metaphor		
Personification		
Past tense		
Present tense		
Present participles (-ing verbs)		

AO2 Looking more closely at structure and form

 ACTIVITY 3

1. Why do you think the two-line stanza is separated from the rest of the poem's stanzas?
2. What do you think Owen is trying to suggest by creating stanzas of uneven length?
3. How does Owen use punctuation to change the mood and pace in the second stanza?

Thinking about themes

 ACTIVITY 4

What do you think Owen's attitude to war is in the poem? Find evidence from the final stanza of the poem to support your views.

 **Developing your own individual response**

ACTIVITY 5

1. Why do you think Owen chose 'Dulce et Decorum Est' as the title for the poem? How suitable a title do you think this is? Suggest an alternative title and explain the reasons for your choice.

2. What do you think is the most horrific line in the poem? Explain your choice.

3. How do you respond to this poem? After reading this poem, would you have been persuaded to enlist to fight the enemy? Write your opinion in a paragraph and include at least two quotations to support your views.

4. Has this poem changed the way in which you think about war and death? Explain your opinion by referring to details from the poem.

 TIP

When reading a poem, remember to read to the punctuation mark rather than to the end of the line. This will help you make more sense of the poem and it will be easier to work out what is happening.

Self-assessment

 ## ACTIVITY 6

Answer true or false to the following statements.

I can comment on and find evidence for how:

- Owen uses language to communicate his feelings about war and death
- Owen uses structure and form to present his ideas
- the poem relates to the context in which it was written.

Working on exam skills

 ACTIVITY 7

Look at this example of an exam-style question:

> Consider how Wilfred Owen writes about war in the poem 'Dulce et Decorum Est'. Use examples from the poem to support your answer.

Choose three of the quotations below. Use them to write three short paragraphs in which you give your own individual response to the poem and write about the effects of language and techniques.

Bent double, like old beggars under sacks,
Knock-kneed, coughing like hags, we cursed through sludge,

Drunk with fatigue; deaf even to the hoots
Of gas-shells dropping softly behind.

Dim, through the misty panes and thick green light,
As under a green sea, I saw him drowning.

In all my dreams, before my helpless sight,
He plunges at me, guttering, choking, drowning.

 ACTIVITY 8

Annotate your answer to show where you have:

- started each paragraph with a clear point
- focused on particular word choices
- explained the effect of the quotations used.

 ACTIVITY 9

Look at the Assessment Objectives on p. 5.

- Which criteria do you think you have shown in your answer?
- What do you think you need to do to improve your performance?

If you think you need to add anything to your paragraphs from Activity 7, redraft them now.

Compare with...

'Dulce et Decorum Est' could be compared with: 'The Manhunt'; 'The Soldier'; 'Mametz Wood'.

'Ozymandias' by Percy Bysshe Shelley

OBJECTIVES

▶ To explore and develop your response to 'Ozymandias' by Percy Bysshe Shelley.

▶ To understand how Shelley has used language, structure and form to express his feelings about power.

▶ To understand some of the contexts of the poem.

Introduction

The poem describes the ruined statue, found in a desert, of a once great and powerful king.

AO3 Context

Percy Bysshe Shelley (1792–1822) was one of the English Romantic poets, along with Blake, Wordsworth, Coleridge, Keats and Byron.

Shelley was thought to be a 'radical' (someone who is revolutionary and untraditional in his thinking) for his time. 'Ozymandias' is about the remains of a statue of the Egyptian Pharaoh Rameses II who built extravagant temples to himself. Shelley's criticism of people who act as if they are invincible is inherent in the poem.

Percy Bysshe Shelley.

Glossary

Ozymandias – the Egyptian pharaoh (ruler) Ramesses II; during his reign he built more temples and monuments than any other pharaoh; he wanted to build memorials for himself that he thought would last forever

antique – ancient

vast – great/huge

trunkless – a pair of legs without a body

visage – face

sculptor – someone who makes a sculpture or statue

pedestal – base for the statue

ye – you

AO1 First thoughts

ACTIVITY 1

1. Can you think of any statues of famous people that have been built? Why do you think they might have been built? Would your attitude change if you thought the famous person had ordered the building of their statue?

2. How many different voices do you think you can hear in the poem? What are they?

3. Read the poem aloud. Try using different tones of voice to create a mood you think is suitable. What sort of atmosphere do you think the poet wants to create?

AO2 Looking more closely at words and images

ACTIVITY 2

1. Which of the following words do you think best describe the personality of Ozymandias as a ruler? Back up your ideas with evidence from the poem.

proud	contemptuous	sympathetic	intelligent	kind
vain	arrogant	gracious	egotistical	charismatic
tyrannical	caring	disdainful	confident	compassionate
modest	callous	tender	conceited	

2. Which words does the poet use to suggest the decay and deterioration that have affected the statue? Annotate each one in as much detail as possible. Here is an example to help you.

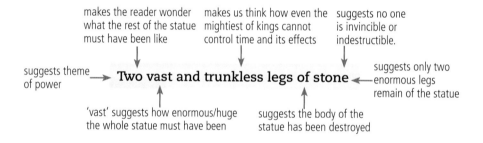

AO2 Looking more closely at structure and form

ACTIVITY 3

1. The poem is written in the form of a 14-line sonnet although it does not have the rhyme scheme and punctuation of most sonnets. What sort of atmosphere do you think the rhyming of 'decay' and 'away' at the ends of lines 12 and 14 helps to create? Do you think this is an appropriate atmosphere for the ending of the poem? Explain your reasons by referring to the words of the poem.

2. How does Shelley use punctuation in the inscription to suggest the superior and contemptuous attitude of Ozymandias?

ACTIVITY 4

Thinking about themes

(1) Copy and complete the table below. Which list is longer? What do you think this is suggesting about Shelley's thoughts about power?

Words suggesting Ozymandias' power	Words suggesting Ozymandias has no power/has been forgotten
sneer	trunkless
cold command	half sunk

(2) Ozymandias' quote suggests hubris (extreme pride or self-confidence). What do you think the poet is suggesting about this theme?

(3) Write down the lines that refer to the sculptor. The only remains of Ozymandias are the inscription and part of his ruined body. The sculptor created these things. What do you think the poet is suggesting about the power of words and art here? Remember to explain your answer by referring to words in the poem.

AO1 Developing your own individual response

 ACTIVITY 5

(1) How do you think Ozymandias' people felt about him? Use evidence from the poem to support your opinions.

(2) Who do you think is the most powerful character in the poem? Explain your answer by referring to evidence from the poem.

(3) How would you sum up your response to the poem in three words?

 TIP

Remember to avoid simply 'spotting' or listing the techniques a poet has used. Always explain the effect these techniques have on a reader.

Self-assessment

 ACTIVITY 6

Answer true or false to the following statements.

I can comment on and find evidence for how Shelley:

● presents the theme of power

● uses language, structure and form to write about the passing of time.

If you answered 'false' to either of the statements, read the poem again and use your answers to the questions on these pages to help you.

Working on exam skills

 ACTIVITY 7

Look at this example of an exam-style question.

> How does Shelley write about the theme of power in 'Ozymandias'?

Write a section on language and imagery that you could include in your answer. Remember to:

- Make a clear point.
- Use evidence from the poem to support your point.
- Explain the effect of the evidence/quotations you have used.
- Focus on particular word choices.

 ACTIVITY 8

Now read the following paragraph written by a student.

Shelley writes about the temporary nature of power in 'Ozymandias' by showing there is a finite limit to his influence. In fact the poem could be interpreted as a metaphor for the ephemeral nature of political power, as the real power lies with the sculptor who has created the 'colossal wreck'. Shelley seems to be implying that art and the written word (suggested by the inscription) have more power over politics as they outlast the reign and power of even the most arrogant 'king of kings'. The image of the 'two vast and trunkless legs' is striking in that it was once a huge statue and we are aware of how powerful Ozymandias once was. However, now he lies 'boundless and bare' on the 'lone' sands in a heap of rubble and abandoned in the desert.

Find examples of where:

- this paragraph begins with a clear point
- the student uses evidence from the poem
- the student explains the effect of the quotations used
- the student focuses on particular word choices.

ACTIVITY 9

After reading the sample answer, if you think you need to add anything to your paragraphs from Activity 7, redraft them now.

Look at the Assessment Objectives on p. 5.

- Which criteria do you think you have shown in your answer?
- What do you think you need to do to improve your performance?

Compare with…

'Ozymandias' could be compared with: 'Hawk Roosting'; 'To Autumn'; 'As Imperceptibly as Grief'.

The toppling of the statue of the dictator Saddam Hussein in Baghdad in 2003

'Mametz Wood' by Owen Sheers

OBJECTIVES

▶ To explore and develop your response to 'Mametz Wood' by Owen Sheers.

▶ To understand how Sheers uses language, structure and form to present death.

▶ To understand some of the contexts of the poem.

Introduction

The poem describes how farmers in France find the bodies of soldiers who were killed in World War I when they are ploughing their fields.

AO3 Context

The Battle of Mametz Wood was one of the bloodiest battles of World War I. The battle began on 7 July 1916, and the generals believed it would be over in a matter of hours. It actually lasted for five days. The 38th Welsh Division suffered terrible loss of life, with 46 officers and 556 soldiers killed. However, when the wounded and those listed as 'missing' (men blown to pieces or buried alive by shell blast) were counted, the total number of British casualties rose to 3,993. The bravery and sacrifice of the soldiers was never really acknowledged.

AO1 First thoughts

ACTIVITY 1

(1) What is your immediate reaction to the poem? What questions might you like to ask about the poem?

(2) What general mood and atmosphere does the poem create?

(3) What are your first impressions of the way in which Sheers presents death? Choose three words or phrases as examples.

Glossary

chit – a small piece of paper

mimicked – imitated/ made fun of

flint – a hard grey rock

sentinel – a guard/sentry

mosaic – a design made of small pieces of coloured stone or glass

relic – part of a dead holy person or a possession belonging to someone holy

dance macabre – a medieval idea of the Dance of Death where a skeleton leads people to their graves

AO2 Looking more closely at words and images

ACTIVITY 2

1 In stanza two, Sheers describes the dead soldiers using a series of metaphors, listed below. Annotate each quote in as much detail as you can. An example is given to help you.

'the chit of bone'

'the relic of a finger'

'the broken bird's egg of a skull'

'the china plate of a shoulder blade' ◄——

A 'china plate' is easily broken and cannot be repaired.
Soldiers' bones are delicate and fragile; they too were easily broken and could not be repaired.

2 In stanza three the soldiers were told 'to walk not run'. Who do you think gave this instruction? What is your opinion about this command? What do you think is the poet's attitude towards this?

3 Pick out some of the words and phrases the poet uses to describe the land, and explain the impressions that are created. You might want to copy out and complete this grid to help you organise your ideas.

Quote	Impression created
As they tended the land back into itself	
The earth stands sentinel	

4 Stanza five creates a very graphic and gruesome picture of the dead soldiers. Pick out the words that you consider to be the most emotive and explain your response to them.

5 What do you think is happening in the last stanza? What do you think the poet is trying to tell us about his feelings here?

 **Looking more closely at structure and form**

📄 ACTIVITY 3

(1) The poet concentrates on a different aspect of the event in each stanza. Sketch out a quick flow chart or mind map to represent the changing focus of each stanza.

(2) Although there is no specific rhyme scheme in the poem, the poet makes great use of assonance and alliteration to create effect. Pick out some examples of these techniques in the poem and write about the effects you think the sounds create.

(3) The poet has used enjambment in some of the lines. Find some examples of where he has used this, and explain the effect it creates.

Thinking about themes

📄 ACTIVITY 4

(1) In the second line, the poet refers to the dead soldiers as 'the wasted young'. What do you think this suggests about his attitude and one of the themes of the poem? Look for some more words and phrases that could be linked to the same theme.

(2) The poem describes how the dead soldiers have been buried beneath the earth and forgotten but are now being discovered by the farmers. What do you think the poet is suggesting about history and the importance of Mametz Wood?

(3) The poet makes several references to nature in the poem. Find examples of where he does this, and think about what he is suggesting about the relationship between man and nature.

AO1 Developing your own individual response

 **ACTIVITY 5**

(1) Pick out one word or phrase from each stanza that has affected you in some way. Explain your choice in each case.

(2) How did you respond to these lines? What do you think the poet means by them?

> their skeletons paused mid dance macabre
>
> in boots that outlasted them

(3) Has this poem changed the way in which you think about war and death? Explain your opinion by referring to details from the poem.

 TIP

Structure your answer clearly by dealing with one idea at a time. Support each point you make with specific reference to the poem.

Self-assessment

 **ACTIVITY 6**

Answer true or false to the following statements.

I can comment on and find evidence for how:

- Sheers uses language to communicate his feelings about war and death
- Sheers uses structure and form to present his ideas
- the poem relates to the context in which it was written.

Working on exam skills

 ACTIVITY 7

Look at this example of an exam-style question:

> Consider how Owen Sheers writes about war in the poem 'Mametz Wood'. Use examples from the poem to support your answer.

Choose three of the quotations below and use them to write three short paragraphs in which you give your own individual response to the poem and write about the effects of its language and techniques.

> the relic of a finger, the blown
> and broken bird's egg of a skull,

> all mimicked now in flint, breaking blue in white
> across this field where they were told to walk, not run

> And even now the earth stands sentinel,
> reaching back into itself for reminders of what happened
> like a wound working a foreign body to the surface of the skin

> As if the notes they had sung
> have only now, with this unearthing,
> slipped from their absent tongues.

 ACTIVITY 8

Annotate your answer to show where you have:

- started each paragraph with a clear point
- focused on particular word choices
- explained the effect of the quotations used.

 ACTIVITY 9

Look at the Assessment Objectives on p. 5.

- Which criteria do you think you have shown in your answer?
- What do you think you need to do to improve your performance?

If you need to add anything to your paragraphs from Activity 7, redraft them now.

Compare with...
'Mametz Wood' could be compared with: 'The Manhunt'; 'The Soldier'; 'A Wife in London'; 'Dulce et Decorum Est'.

'The Prelude' (extract) by William Wordsworth

OBJECTIVES

▶ To explore and develop your response to 'The Prelude' by William Wordsworth.
▶ To understand how William Wordsworth has used language, structure and form to express his feelings about an event.
▶ To understand some of the contexts of the poem.

Introduction

This is an autobiographical poem and in this extract the poet, William Wordsworth, describes skating on a frozen lake just as night is falling.

William Wordsworth (1770–1850) was born and lived in the Lake District, and this background greatly influenced his writing and his appreciation of nature. In this extract from *The Prelude* you can see how the power of nature affected Wordsworth when he was a child.

AO3 Context

In 1796, Wordsworth, along with his sister Dorothy and fellow poet Samuel Taylor Coleridge, worked on a collection of poems which became known as *The Lyrical Ballads*. This collection is very important as it marks the beginning of the Romantic movement in literature. The Romantic movement was popular at the end of the eighteenth century and reflected a change in the way people thought about art and writing. Artists and writers produced work that celebrated nature, emotions and imagination, and they found beauty in the ordinary, everyday world.

Glossary

heeded not – did not pay attention to
rapture – wonder or excitement
toll'd – rang
exulting – joyful or triumphant
Confederate – united
resounding – echoing
tumult – din/commotion

AO1 First thoughts

ACTIVITY 1

① This part of 'The Prelude' begins with Wordsworth describing a childhood memory of skating with friends. Read and track through the 22 lines of the extract, and describe what happens in each section.

(2) This is clearly a very personal experience and one Wordsworth still remembers when he is an adult. Why do you think this is? Find a word/phrase to suggest how personal the experience is.

AO2 Looking more closely at words and images

📄 ACTIVITY 2

(1) Look at these three extracts from the poem. Annotate each one by writing down the effect the words/images have on you. Can you explain what you think Wordsworth means in each case?

> It was a time of rapture: clear and loud
> The village clock toll'd six
>
>   wheel'd about,
> Proud and exulting, like an untir'd horse,
> That cares not for his home.
>
> Meanwhile, the precipices rang aloud,
> The leafless trees, and every icy crag
> Tinkled like iron

(2) Read lines 9 ('all shod with steel') to 15 ('and not a voice was idle'). How does Wordsworth show that he is enjoying the experience at this point? What sort of atmosphere does Wordsworth create in these lines?

(3) In lines 18–22 (from 'while the distant hills' to 'the orange sky of evening died away'), the mood changes. Think about how Wordsworth creates this shift in mood and atmosphere. You might find it helpful to copy and complete the table below to organise your thoughts.

Quote	Effect
the distant hills	
sent an alien sound/Of melancholy	
were sparkling clear	
The orange sky of evening died away	

(4) Do you think Wordsworth's thoughts and feelings have changed by the end of the extract? Find some words and phrases to prove that Wordsworth feels differently by the end of his experience.

AO2 Looking more closely at structure and form

 **ACTIVITY 3**

(1) This extract does not have any stanzas and is written in blank verse. Why do you think Wordsworth decided to do this, and what is the effect of this?

(2) There is a very conversational tone to the extract, with the words 'and', 'indeed', 'so' and 'meanwhile'. What effect do you think this has on the reader?

(3) 'The Prelude' is sometimes described as an 'epic' poem because of its length. Epic poems usually describe events that have a lot of action. Here Wordsworth writes about ordinary events. Can you think why these events could be described as 'epic'?

Thinking about themes

ACTIVITY 4

(1) This extract of 'The Prelude' describes nature as something that can change. Can you find evidence in the poem of how Wordsworth suggests the ideas of change and transition?

(2) Wordsworth, as part of the Romantic Movement, was always in awe of the beauty of nature. How does he present his admiration for nature in this extract? Find some words or phrases to back up your ideas.

(3) Wordsworth is describing an experience about the freedom and excitement of youth. Find some words to show how he presents the ideas of excitement and youth here.

 # Developing your own individual response

 ## ACTIVITY 5

 TIP

(1) Have you noticed the way in which Wordsworth uses references to darkness and light in the poem? Pick out some of these images. Decide which image you think is the most effective, and give reasons for your choice.

(2) You will have noticed that Wordsworth uses personification, sibilance, juxtaposition and similes in this part of 'The Prelude'. Find examples of where he does this. Choose your favourite examples of these techniques and explain why you have chosen them.

> When you are writing about poems, there is no point in just trying to 'spot' different techniques. The examiners will be more impressed if you can <u>explain</u> the <u>effects</u> of these techniques. Remember it is more useful to explain why you think a poet has chosen a particular word or phrase than to 'spot' lots of different techniques.

Self-assessment

ACTIVITY 6

Answer true or false to the following statements.

I can comment on and find evidence for how:

- Wordsworth presents a sense of excitement in the extract
- nature affects Wordsworth in the extract
- Wordsworth uses language to communicate his experience
- Wordsworth's ideas reflect the themes of the Romantic movement in this extract.

Working on exam skills

 ACTIVITY 7

Look at this example of an exam-style question.

> How does Wordsworth present nature in this extract from 'The Prelude'? Use examples from the poem to support your answer.

Write a section on how Wordsworth uses words and images that you could include in your answer. You may find it helpful to include some of these words in your answer:

powerful   exciting   autobiographical   transition

freedom   nostalgic   energy

Remember to:

- Respond to the text.
- Comment on the way the poet has used language, form and structure to create meaning and effect.
- Show you understand the period when the poem was written.

 ACTIVITY 8

When you have finished, read the following paragraph written by a student.

> Wordsworth expresses his feelings of admiration and awe for nature by describing his autobiographical childhood experience of skating with friends. Just like other poets of the Romantic period, Wordsworth admires the simple beauty of nature and describes some of his observations in detail so we can share his admiration and excitement. For example, he even notices the 'stars' were 'sparkling clear' and 'the orange sky of evening'. He also writes about how his impression of nature can change. For example, he later describes nature as being quite sinister and threatening when, 'the precipices rang aloud' and 'every icy crag tinkled like iron'. Words like 'leafless', 'iron' and 'icy' create a barren impression in keeping perhaps with a winter landscape.

Find examples of where:

- clear points are made
- the student uses evidence from the poem
- the student explains the effect of the quotations used
- the student focuses on particular word choices.

 ACTIVITY 9

Compare what you have written with this sample answer. If you need to add anything to your paragraphs from Activity 7, redraft them.

Now write a section on how Wordsworth uses structure and form in this part of 'The Prelude'.

Compare with...

'The Prelude' could be compared with: 'To Autumn'; 'London'; 'Death of a Naturalist'; 'Afternoons'.

Approaching the examination

In Section B part (b) of Component 1 you will be asked to write about a second poem of your choice from the WJEC Eduqas Poetry Anthology and to compare it with the poem in the first question.

In the poems that you are comparing, you should be able to compare what they are about (content); how they are organised (structure); how the writers create effects (language, techniques and word choices); and the contexts of the poems.

Planning your comparison is going to be vital if you want to score highly. You might want to list the ideas and features you are going to compare and then jot down the details and quotes that you intend to use to support the points you will make.

Preparation is the key to success here! Long before you take your exam, you need to become familiar with the kinds of question that you may be asked.

Here are some sample questions:

> Compare the presentation of power in your chosen poem to the presentation of power in 'Ozymandias'.
>
> Compare how the poets write about the passing of time in your chosen poem and in 'Afternoons'.

Now think about which poems could be compared and contrasted, and practise making up four exam-style questions of your own.

How can I do well in Section B part (b) of Component 1?

The examination is your opportunity to put into practice and show off all the skills you have been practising in these activities. Now your next challenge is to work out how to organise and structure your response to score the highest marks you can. You might find it helpful to follow this plan of action.

- **Read** the question very carefully. Underline or highlight the key words in the question and decide what it is exactly that you are being asked to do.

TIP

Always choose a poem that gives you the most scope to make a range of comparisons with the named poem in part (a).

- **Plan** carefully and take a few minutes to decide which poem you will choose to make your comparison. This decision will be vital because you must make sure that you have enough to write about! For example, you might decide to write about your favourite or the most similar poem. To achieve a mark in Band 5, you will have to produce a comparison that is 'critical, illuminating and sustained across all three Assessment Objectives'. This suggests it would be sensible to draw up a quick list of similarities and differences before you start writing; **however**, it does not mean that every point you make has to be compared! Jot down some of the key ideas and themes from both poems and a few of the details you might want to explore and analyse. Do not panic about your timing. This is time well spent, and five minutes planning time here will ensure that your writing is coherent, focused and detailed.

- **Write** with confidence! You should aim to write about the content, themes, language, structure and contexts of the poems. This might sound daunting but remember to be **selective**! You will not be able or be expected to cover every single thing you know about the poems in the time allowed – write about the poems in the ways you have practised in this section. But do remember to write enough about the second poem!

- **Check** your work if you have any time left at the end of the examination, and decide whether you could improve your answer in any way. For example, could you add another sentence to explain the effect of a particular word or image? Could you make another point about the context of the poems? Could you include an extra sentence to describe your reaction to the poem? Making improvements like this might score you an extra mark or two! Remember to check that you have covered all the Assessment Objectives in your answer. Do not worry about checking errors in spelling or punctuation because they do not carry any marks in this section.

Now it is time to practise planning an exam response.

Here is an exam-style question:

> Compare the presentation of nature in your chosen poem to the presentation of nature in 'To Autumn'.

There are a few poems you could choose for this comparison but let's say that you choose 'Death of a Naturalist' – this poem explores a child's excitement in his discovery of the natural world, whereas 'To Autumn' is about the poet's feelings of admiration for the season.

Look at this example of a quick plan written by a student in response to this question.

> **1) Theme**
>
> 'Death' – passing of time; change/transformation/loss of innocence
>
> 'To Autumn' – passing of time with some images of death at the end

> **2) Language, structure and form**
>
> 'Death' – adjectives, use of contrast, onomatopoeia and effects; child-like imagery and appeal to senses
>
> 'To Autumn' – personification, adjectives, rhetorical questions and effects

> **3) Contexts**
>
> 'Death' – twentieth-century Irish rural setting; autobiographical element
>
> 'To Autumn'– pastoral, rural setting; autobiographical element
>
> Importance of natural world to both poets

The words in this plan have been written in full, but in timed exam conditions it might be a good idea to abbreviate some words. As you can see, the student has selected a few key areas to concentrate on and has numbered the order in which the points are to be covered. What else do you think the student might have found helpful to jot down quickly in the plan? Has the plan focused on all the Assessment Objectives?

Comparing the poems in the Anthology

OBJECTIVES:

▶ To compare poems and address the Assessment Objectives.
▶ To develop and improve your writing skills.
▶ To practise exam-style questions and writing under timed conditions.

In Section B of Component 1 you will be asked to write about **two** poems from the WJEC Eduqas Poetry Anthology.

In Section B part (a) you will be asked to write about a named poem from the Anthology that will be printed on the exam paper for you. Here you will be expected to address the following Assessment Objectives in your response:

● AO1: responding to the poem with your own ideas and thoughts.
● AO2: analysing how a poet has used language, structure and form to create meaning and effect.
● AO3: understanding the contexts in which the poem was written.

In Section B part (b) you will be asked to choose and write about **one** other poem from the Anthology which is similar in content, theme or form to the poem in part (a). Here you will be expected to focus on the same Assessment Objectives in your response.

In addition to these Assessment Objectives, you must be aware that you also need to write about comparisons and contrasts between the poems. The list below will help you to understand how the comparative element fits in to each band.

● In **Band 1** comparisons will be very limited. There may be **basic** awareness of the obvious similarities and/or differences between the poems.
● In **Band 2** comparisons will be general with **some** discussion of the obvious similarities and/or differences between the poems.
● In **Band 3** comparisons will be focused with some **valid** discussion of the similarities and/or differences between the poems.

- In **Band 4** comparisons will be focused, coherent and sustained with **clear** discussion of the similarities and/or differences between the poems.
- In **Band 5** comparisons will be critical, illuminating and sustained with **wide-ranging** discussion of the similarities and/or differences between the poems.

So, for example, if the named and printed poem in part (a) was 'Afternoons' by Philip Larkin, and there was a question about relationships in part (b), you could choose to write about 'Sonnet 43', 'Cozy Apologia' or 'Valentine'.

The poems could be compared in terms of content, theme and form and, as you may have noticed already, many poems may have more than one theme. For this reason it is worth considering which poems could be linked.

The following table (based on the 18 poems in the Anthology) has been started for you to help you organise your thoughts and draw comparisons between the poems.

Copy and complete the table. You can place the poems in more than one category. You can add more rows for any other ideas or themes you feel could connect the poems.

Ideas	Poem(s)
Death	'The Manhunt', 'The Soldier', 'A Wife in London', 'Dulce et Decorum Est', 'Mametz Wood'
Place/location	'London', 'Living Space', 'The Prelude'
War	'The Manhunt', 'Mametz Wood'
Relationships	'The Manhunt', 'Valentine'
Grief	'A Wife in London', 'The Soldier'
Nature	'As Imperceptibly as Grief', 'To Autumn', 'Death of a Naturalist', 'The Prelude'
Power	'Hawk Roosting', 'Ozymandias'
Seasons	'To Autumn'
Love	'Afternoons'
The passing of time	'Ozymandias'
Admiration and awe	'She Walks in Beauty'
The fragility of life	'Living Space'
Sonnet	'Sonnet 43'
Change or transformation	'Death of a Naturalist'

What does comparison actually mean?

Comparison simply means that you should show how the poems are **similar** and also how the poems are **different**. If you **contrast** as well as **compare**, you will have more to write about.

Making the right choice!

 ACTIVITY 1

Think about how to tackle a comparison question.

Look at this exam-style question:

> Compare the presentation of love in your chosen poem to the presentation of love in 'Valentine'.

Think about which poem you might want to use. Write down a list of the poems you think would be the most suitable choices.

Starting off

 ACTIVITY 2

Let's use 'Sonnet 43' as the comparison poem.

Begin by writing a sentence or two about each poem, summing up what the poem is about and each writer's attitude towards relationships.

Focus on language

 ACTIVITY 3

Think about how Elizabeth Barrett Browning uses language to achieve specific effects, and how this compares to Carol Ann Duffy's use of language in 'Valentine'.

Look at the phrases at the top of the next page which Barrett Browning uses to suggest her feelings about love and relationships. For each quotation, say why you think the poet chose it and how she uses it to make her point about love and relationships.

 TIP

The question is worth 25 marks, so you need to make sure that you allow an appropriate amount of time to answer the question. It is suggested that you allow one hour to complete the poetry questions. It might be a good idea to spend 20 minutes on the first task which is worth 15 marks, then 40 minutes on the second part of the task because it is worth 25 marks.

Skills for Literature and the Unseen Poetry Student's Book

'to the level of every day's/Most quiet need'

'I love thee freely, as men strive for Right'

'I love thee with a love I seemed to lose/With my lost saints'

'I love thee with the breath/Smiles, tears, of all my life!'

In 'Valentine' Duffy uses images to suggest her feelings about love and relationships. Think about why she has selected each of the images below and how she has used each image to make her points about love.

'Not a red rose or a satin heart'

'an onion/Wrapped in brown paper'

'its fierce kiss will stay on your lips'

'its platinum loops shrink to a wedding ring'

What do you notice about the similarities and differences in the words chosen by the poets?

How the poems are built

 ACTIVITY 4

Compare the structure and form of the two poems by writing a couple of sentences about each of the following points:
- The form of each poem and how the stanzas are organised.
- The use of a speaker or narrator in the poem.
- The use of punctuation for effect.
- The use of rhyme and/or rhythm.
- How the poet hooks the reader's attention from the start.

Remembering contexts

 ACTIVITY 5

What do the contexts of each poem suggest about the attitudes of the poets?

Your opinion counts!

 ACTIVITY 6

Think about your reaction to each poem and how each one affects you. For each poem write a few sentences about the features and how they create that effect on you.

Choosing suitable examples

 ACTIVITY 7

Copy and complete the table below to help you compare the two poems. Remember to include evidence and quotes from both poems.

Poem	Language	Structure	Contexts
'Sonnet 43'			
'Valentine'			

Choose six quotations from the poems to support each of the sections in the table.

Structuring your response

 ACTIVITY 8

Now read the following paragraphs written by a student in response to this exam-style question:

> Compare the presentation of love in your chosen poem to the presentation of love in 'Valentine'.

'Sonnet 43' is written in the first person and it focuses on the all-consuming intensity of the poet's love for her husband-to-be. However the subject matter of 'Valentine' is much more grounded and realistic, as Duffy describes how she would rather give an 'onion' as a Valentine gift instead of the conventional and traditional 'satin heart'.

At the start of 'Sonnet 43' the poet asks her lover, 'How do I love thee? Let me count the ways' and she goes on to show the different ways in which she loves him. In the spatial metaphor 'to the depth and breadth and height/My soul can reach', the poet is suggesting that love is something that is filling her soul completely and that her love cannot be restricted or confined. However, she also loves him in a more realistic and domestic way, 'to the level of every day's/Most quiet need'. Although her need might be 'quiet' it is no less deep, and the reference to 'by sun and candlelight' emphasises how she loves him day and night.

In contrast, in 'Valentine' we see Duffy focus on one main image to describe her love – an 'onion'. Here the poet's attitude to love is more challenging and cynical as the 'onion' has positive and negative qualities, and perhaps Duffy is trying to tell us that is exactly what love is like – both love and the onion 'will blind you with tears'.

Find and write down examples of where the student has:

- made a clear point
- used quotations
- explained the effect of quotations
- focused closely on language
- used words and phrases that show comparison.

On your own!

 ACTIVITY 9

Now try writing five or six paragraphs giving your response to a different exam-style question:

> Compare the presentation of place or location in one poem of your choice from the Anthology to the presentation of place in 'London'.

When you have finished, read through your response and annotate your paragraphs using the checklist from Activity 8. If you think you need to add anything else to your response or you need to improve it in any way, do it now. Using the Assessment Objectives on p. 5, decide which band you think your paragraphs would fall into.

 TIP

Remember to check that you have written about the contexts of the poems.

Comparing ideas and themes – further practice

 **ACTIVITY 1**

Read the poems 'Dulce et Decorum Est' and 'The Soldier'.

Starting off

 ACTIVITY 2

Write down as many similarities and differences as you can find between these poems. You could use a Venn diagram like the one below if this is easier.

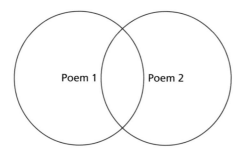

For example, both poems are about war and although they are both set in World War I, 'The Soldier' was written at the start of the war whereas 'Dulce et Decorum Est' was written in 1917 towards the end of the war.

Beginning to compare themes

 ACTIVITY 3

Now look at your list of similarities and differences. Try to make your ideas and annotations a bit more specific.

For example:

- Although both poems are written in the first person, can you detect a different tone and attitude from each speaker?
- Although both poems are about death, do they consider death in the same way?

For each point you think of, remember to select a relevant quotation or piece of evidence from the poems in support.

Comparing writers' methods and structure

 ACTIVITY 4

When you are confident that you have compared the content, themes and attitudes in both poems, you need to start thinking about similarities and differences in the methods the poets use and the effects they achieve.

For example:

- What do you notice about the descriptions in each poem? Are the images in the poems equally gruesome and graphic?
- Do both poems have the same form and structure?
- Can you find any significance in the titles of the two poems?

Make a list of as many similarities and differences in the methods used in the poems as you can. Try to find a few details or quotations that are similar or different, and write about the effects they create.

Putting your skills into practice

 ACTIVITY 5

Look at these quotes:

> There shall be/In that rich earth a richer dust concealed
> **['The Soldier']**

> In all my dreams, before my helpless sight,
> He plunges at me, guttering, choking, drowning
> **['Dulce et Decorum Est']**

Think about and explore the similarities and differences between these quotes.

After completing all of these activities, you should have found plenty of ideas to help you write a detailed comparison of the poems. Remember that you need to choose the details wisely to make sure that you have enough to write about!

The unseen poems: Introduction

How does this part of the book work?

This part of the book has been designed to help you improve your skills, develop your confidence and raise your achievement in the WJEC Eduqas GCSE English Literature Component 2 examination. In this exam you will be writing about poems you have not studied previously in class.

In this section you will:

- Improve your understanding of the theme or message and mood of previously unseen poems.
- Develop your own individual response to an unseen poem.
- Write about the similarities and differences between unseen poems.
- Look at sample answers representing different levels of achievement and mark them against the Assessment Objectives and marking criteria.
- Reflect on your own understanding and work out how to improve your performance.
- Look at exam-style questions and practise writing exam-style responses.
- Judge your own performance by marking your responses against the Assessment Objectives and marking criteria.

Assessment Objectives

What do they really mean? The simple truth!

Assessment Objectives are the criteria or standards that will be used when you write about poems that you have not previously studied for the unseen poetry section.

In Component 2 Section C parts (a) and (b) you will be assessed only on AO1 and AO2.

Here is a reminder of what the Assessment Objectives are actually asking you to do.

AO1 is the objective where you give your own personal response to what you have read and how you show it.

AO1 says 'read, understand and respond to texts'. This just means that you will be reading the poems and showing that you understand them by saying what you think they are about and what some of the details mean.

AO1 says 'maintain a critical style and develop an informed personal response.' This means you need to think about what the poets want to communicate and show how they do this.

AO1 says 'use textual reference, including quotes to support and illustrate interpretations'. For this you need to use evidence and examples from the poems to prove your points. You can quote by picking out words from the poems to support your opinions.

AO2 is the objective where you need to look at the poets' craft and how language is used to create effects.

AO2 says 'analyse language, form and structure used by a writer to create meaning and effects'. It is probably easier to break this down and think about the objective in terms of three things:
- **Language** – write about the way the poets use words, images and techniques to create effects.
- **Form** – this could be the types of poem the poets have chosen to write, such as a sonnet or a ballad, or specific things like rhyme and rhythm.
- **Structure** – this is the way the poets have decided to organise their ideas. You could think about the way the poets have organised the whole poem or particular stanzas. Sometimes poems have a circular structure where the ending refers back to the first stanza.

AO2 says 'using subject terminology where appropriate'. Be careful not to treat this as a feature-spotting hunt! It is much more important to write about the effect the words have rather than to know the correct terminology, although you should use the terminology if you know it.

Assessment Objectives for Section C Part (a)

For Part (a) you will be writing about a single poem that you have not studied previously.

There will be 15 marks available for this question. You will be assessed on AO1 and AO2 and they are worth equal marks.

Here are the marking criteria for this question. Notice that the key words in each band have been written in bold so you can see at a glance the progression of skills.

Band	AO1	AO2
Band 5 **(13–15 marks)**	You **sustain focus** on the task, including an **overview**, convey ideas with **consistent coherence** and use an **appropriate register**; use a **sensitive and evaluative** approach to the task and **analyse the text critically**; show a **perceptive understanding** of the text, engaging perhaps with some **originality** in your personal response; your responses should include **pertinent, direct references** from across the text, including quotations.	You **analyse** and **appreciate** writers' use of language, form and structure; make **assured reference** to meanings and effects, **exploring and evaluating** the way meaning and ideas are conveyed through language, structure and form; use **precise subject terminology** in an appropriate context.
Band 4 **(10–12 marks)**	You **sustain focus** on the task, convey ideas with **coherence** and use an **appropriate register**; use a **thoughtful approach** to the task; show a **secure understanding** of key aspects of the text, with **considerable engagement**; support and justify your responses by **well-chosen direct reference** to the text, including quotations.	You **discuss and increasingly analyse** writers' use of language, form and structure; make **thoughtful reference** to the meanings and effects of stylistic features used by the writer; use **apt subject terminology**.

Band	AO1	AO2
Band 3 **(7–9 marks)**	You focus on the task, convey ideas with general coherence and use a mostly appropriate register; use a straightforward approach to the task; show an understanding of key aspects of the text, with engagement; support and justify your responses by appropriate direct reference to the text, including quotations.	You comment on and begin to evaluate writers' use of language, form and structure; make some reference to meanings and effects; use relevant subject terminology.
Band 2 **(4–6 marks)**	You have some focus on the task, convey ideas with some coherence and sometimes use an appropriate register; use a limited approach to the task; show some understanding of key aspects of the text, with some engagement; support and justify your responses by some direct reference to the text, including some quotations.	You recognise and make simple comments on writers' use of language, form and structure; may make limited reference to meanings and effects; may use some relevant terminology.
Band 1 **(1–3 marks)**	You have limited focus on the task, convey ideas with occasional coherence and may sometimes use an appropriate register; use a simple approach to the task; show a basic understanding of some key aspects of the text, with a little engagement; may support and justify your responses by some general reference to the text, perhaps including some quotations.	You may make generalised comments on writers' use of language, form and structure; make basic reference to meanings and effects; may use some subject terminology but not always accurately or appropriately.

Assessment Objectives for Section C Part (b)

For Part (b) you will be writing about a second poem that you have not studied previously and linking it to the unseen poem in part (a).

There will be 25 marks available for this question. You will be assessed on AO1 and AO2, and they are worth equal marks.

Here are the marking criteria for this question. Notice that the key words in each band have been written in bold so you can see at a glance the progression of skills.

Band	AO1	AO2	Summary
Band 5 (21–5 marks)	You **sustain focus** on the task, **including an overview**, convey ideas with **consistent coherence** and use an appropriate register; use a **sensitive and evaluative** approach to the task and **analyse the text critically**; show a **perceptive understanding** of the text, engaging perhaps **with some originality** in your personal response; your responses should include **pertinent, direct references** from across the text, including quotations.	You **analyse and appreciate** writers' use of language, form and structure; make **assured reference to meanings and effects, exploring and evaluating** the way meaning and ideas are conveyed through language, structure and form; use **precise subject terminology** in an appropriate context.	In this band comparison is **critical, illuminating and sustained**. There will be a **wide-ranging** discussion of the similarities and/or differences between the poems.
Band 4 (16–20 marks)	You **sustain focus** on the task, convey ideas with **coherence** and use an appropriate register; use a **thoughtful** approach to the task; show a **secure understanding** of key aspects of the text, with **considerable engagement**; support and justify your responses by **well-chosen direct reference** to the text, including quotations.	You **discuss and increasingly analyse** writers' use of language, form and structure; make **thoughtful reference** to the meanings and effects of stylistic features used by the writer; use **apt subject terminology**.	In this band comparison is **focused, coherent and sustained**. There will be a **clear** discussion of the similarities and/or differences between the poems.

Band	AO1	AO2	Summary
Band 3 (11–15 marks)	You focus on the task, convey ideas with general coherence and use a mostly appropriate register; use a straightforward approach to the task; show an understanding of key aspects of the text, with engagement; support and justify your responses by appropriate direct reference to the text, including quotations.	You comment on and begin to evaluate writers' use of language, form and structure; make some reference to meanings and effects; use relevant subject terminology.	In this band, comparison is focused with some valid discussion of the similarities and/ or differences between the poems.
Band 2 (6–10 marks)	You have some focus on the task, convey ideas with some coherence and sometimes use an appropriate register; use a limited approach to the task; show some understanding of key aspects of the text, with some engagement; support and justify your responses by some direct reference to the text, including some quotations.	You recognise and make simple comments on writers' use of language, form and structure; may make limited reference to meanings and effects; may use some relevant terminology.	In this band comparison is general with some discussion of the obvious similarities and/or differences between the poems.
Band 1 (1–5 marks)	You have limited focus on the task, convey ideas with occasional coherence and may sometimes use an appropriate register; use a simple approach to the task; show a basic understanding of some key aspects of the text, with a little engagement; may support and justify your responses by some general reference to the text, perhaps including some quotations.	You may make generalised comments on writers' use of language, form and structure; make basic reference to meanings and effects; may use some subject terminology but not always accurately or appropriately.	In this band comparison is very limited. There may be a basic awareness of the obvious similarities and/or differences between the poems.

Component 2 Section C parts (a) and (b)

What do I need to know about this part of the exam?

You will be taking this exam as part of the WJEC Eduqas GCSE English Literature qualification, so what exactly will you have to do?

The activities in this part of the book are to support your learning for the following section of the exam: **Component 2 Section C – Unseen poetry**

Here are answers to some questions you may have about this part of the exam.

How much is this section worth?

This section is worth 20 per cent of your total mark.

How long should I spend on this section?

You should spend one hour on Section C.

Which Assessment Objectives are assessed in this section?

In Component 2 Section C you will be assessed on AO1 and AO2.

What will each question ask me to do?

You will have to answer both parts of the question: part (a) and part (b).

Part (a) is worth 15 marks. In this part you will be given a single poem to write about.

Part (b) is worth 25 marks. In this part you will be given a second poem to write about and link to the poem in part (a).

Will the poems be modern or old-fashioned?

They will be modern and from the twentieth and/or twenty-first century.

Will marks be allocated to this section for my accuracy in spelling, punctuation and the use of grammar?

No.

Unseen poetry – what will I have to do?

For this part of your English Literature exam, you will have to write about a single 'unseen' poem, and then to write about a second 'unseen' poem and link it to the first poem. Do not panic when you hear the word 'unseen'! It simply means that it is unlikely that you will have previously read, seen or studied these poems. Still feeling a bit apprehensive about it? Then do not worry because you will be given a list of bullet points with the question to help you organise your ideas and structure your response.

The wording of the question for part (a) will look something like this:

> Write about the following poem and its effect on you.
> You may wish to consider:
>
> ▪ what the poem is about and how it is organised
> ▪ the ideas the poet may have wanted us to think about
> ▪ the poet's choice of words, phrases and images and the effects they create
> ▪ how you respond to the poem.

The wording of the question for part (b) will look something like this:

> Now compare both poems.
> You should compare:
>
> ▪ what the poems are about and how they are organised
> ▪ the ideas the poets may have wanted us to think about
> ▪ the poets' choice of words, phrases and images and the effects they create
> ▪ how you respond to the poems.

There are no prescribed texts to study for the unseen poems in Section C. However, poems that are suitable for study to help prepare you for this section of your exam could include those by the following poets:

Fleur Adcock, John Agard, Moniza Alvi, Maya Angelou, Simon Armitage, James Berry, Eavan Boland, Wendy Cope, Tony Curtis, Carol Ann Duffy, Rita Dove, Jen Hadfield, Tony Harrison, Ted Hughes, Jackie Kay, Philip Larkin, Liz Lochead, Roger McGough, Robert Minhinnick, Andrew Motion, Grace Nichols, Sean O'Brien, Seamus Heaney, Adrienne Rich, Jo Shapcott, Owen Sheers, Derek Walcott, William Carlos Williams, Benjamin Zephaniah; and works by other poets from the twentieth and twenty-first centuries.

How do I read an 'unseen' poem?

Top tips for success!

The first tip is not to panic! The poems will have been chosen carefully so that students will be able to give a response to them in timed conditions in an exam. The points below are some suggestions for how to tackle the poems and some questions you should be asking yourself as you read through the poem.

1. Read the poem slowly and carefully, and then re-read it two or three times before you even begin to think about putting pen to paper. Try to 'get a handle' on the general meaning of what is happening in the poem. Remember to read from punctuation mark to punctuation mark, instead of from line to line. This will help you to make sense of the poem.

2. There will always be bullet points with the question to help you focus your ideas. It is a good idea to use them but you can write about them in any order, and you do not have to write the same amount for each one.

3. Always read the line 'introducing' the poem as this may give you an indication as to what the poem may be about. For example, the question might state, 'In both these poems the poets write about the ending of a relationship and the effects it can have on people.'

4. Do not worry if you do not understand every word in the poem. It is worth checking whether any words are starred with an * (asterisk) and explained at the bottom of the page. If not, you may be able to work their meaning out from the general mood of the poem.

5. Think about the poem's title. Sometimes it may have an obvious and self-explanatory meaning, or it may suggest something about the theme and tone of the poem. Try to write something about the title as it is often a 'way in' to the poem, but only if there is something valid to say.

6. Make sure you keep reading and are not tempted to skim the ending of the poem; sometimes you may find a key image or unexpected twist, contrast or surprise at the very end!

(7) When you read the poem for the second time, highlight key words, phrases and images, and start to ask yourself why the poet has chosen to use them. On your third reading, annotate and make some brief notes on the poems about the ideas suggested by the words.

(8) Ask yourself who is speaking in the poem and to whom.

(9) Try to work out the mood and atmosphere created in the poem by looking at key words; for example, there may be many words which would create a gloomy and depressing mood.

(10) Think about what the poet wants the reader to 'take away' from reading the poem. Is there a particular lesson or message you can take from it?

(11) After you have considered all these points, you will have formed quite a strong idea of the poem. Try to form an overall impression of the poem in a couple of sentences.

(12) Have you noticed anything about how the poem is structured? Is it divided into stanzas? Is there any rhyme, and if so, what is the effect?

(13) Remember to give your own individual response to the poem! For example, have you connected with the poem? Has the poem reminded you of a particular experience? Can you identify with the character or situation being described?

Finally ... remember that there is never just one 'right answer' to a poem. You will always be rewarded for your ideas as long as you back them up by using quotations or evidence from the poem. If you want to show the examiner that there could be more than one way of understanding a particular word or phrase, you might find it helpful to use tentative language, such as 'perhaps', 'maybe', 'alternately'.

Working with an 'unseen poem'

▶ To tackle an unseen poem with confidence.
▶ To develop your critical reading skills.

In the exam, when you are faced with poems you have not previously seen, you will need to read them and reach an understanding of them without the help of your teacher. This section of the book will help you to develop the necessary skills to interpret poems on your own and build up your confidence, so that you are ready to face any poem!

Look at this poem.

'Autumn', by Alan Bold

Autumn arrives
Like an experienced robber
Grabbing the green stuff
Then cunningly covering his tracks
With a deep multitude
Of colourful distractions.
And the wind,
The wind is his accomplice
Putting an air of chaos
Into the careful diversions
So branches shake
And dead leaves are suddenly blown
In the faces of strangers.
The theft chills the world
Changes the temper of the earth
Till the normally placid sky
Glows red with a quiet rage.

ACTIVITY 1

Read the poem carefully and make some notes on the following points:
- What you think the poem is about.
- The ideas the poet may have wanted us to think about.
- The mood and atmosphere created.
- Key words or phrases that stand out to you and the effect they have on you.
- Anything you can say about the way the poem is structured or organised.
- Your response to the poem.

 ACTIVITY 2

You may have noticed that the title is self-explanatory, and tells you exactly what the poem is going to be about.

Think about your response to the poem and the notes you have made.
- What ideas did you think the poet wanted you to think about?
- What sort of mood was created? Which words or phrases do you think suggest this?
- Are the key words and phrases that you picked out linked in any way? Try to decide what effect they have on you. What impression of autumn does it create?
- What did you notice about the length of the lines? What effect do you think this has on the poem? Does the final line change the tone of the poem?

If you want to add more points to your notes and ideas about the poem, do it now.

Now that you have had a chance to respond to an unseen poem, let's think about what features are needed to produce a successful written response.

ACTIVITY 3

Here are the opening paragraphs to three different responses on 'Autumn'. Read them carefully and consider the differences between them. Which one do you think is the best and why? Which do you think is least successful?

Student A

The poem is about the autumn and how it comes and leaves a trail of old leaves behind. The poet describes autumn as like a thief using a 'colourful distraction' and giving the air of chaos. The poet may have wanted us to think that he doesn't like autumn and he may prefer us to think that he likes another season better.

Student B

The poem is describing autumn. The poet wants us to think about all the colours we see. The mood is calm and the poem uses descriptive words like describing leaves as 'colourful'.

Student C

The poem is about how quickly autumn comes and how it is 'like an experienced robber' who knows exactly what to do. The idea the poet may have wanted us to think about is how quickly autumn comes and how much it changes our lives. This is shown in the quote, 'the faces of inquisitive strangers'. He also wants us to think about how this all happens under our noses and yet we still don't recognise it because he writes, 'then cunningly covering his tracks' with 'colourful distractions'.

How did you do? If you thought that Student C had written the best introduction, you were right. Here are some of the good features about the response:

- It is quickly focused on what the poem is about.
- It shows an understanding of the poet's intentions.
- It refers to evidence from the poem and integrates the quotes into the sentences.

If you thought Student B had produced the least successful introduction, you were right. Here are some of the reasons why the response was not as successful:

- The comments are straightforward and undeveloped.
- A quote is used but is not explored or probed.

 ## ACTIVITY 4

Now look at the following paragraphs written in response to the same poem about the words and phrases that the students find interesting or effective. Read them carefully and consider the differences between them. Which one do you think is the best and why? Which do you think is least successful?

Student A

The poet describes the wind 'as his accomplice, putting an air of chaos'. It describes the wind like it is a side effect of the autumn. It makes me feel like autumn is an enemy and is evil because the poet compares it to a 'robber' and 'the theft chills the world'. This suggests that autumn is doing this everywhere in the world and to every different culture.

Student B

The poet describes autumn as an 'experienced robber and the wind his accomplice'. This poem creates many images in the reader's mind because of the colours and the verbs he uses. The mood of the poem is fast and energetic.

Student C

The poem tells us that autumn is like an 'experienced robber' who has a lot of colours and 'experience'. It changes the temperature of the earth and the normally 'placid sky' is red with a quiet rage.

How did you do? If you thought Student A was the best response, you were right. Here are some of the good features about the response:

● The points are well made and supported.

● The effects of the words are explained.

If you thought Student C produced the least successful response, you were right. This is because:

● The student has not really selected any key words.

● The understanding and comments are limited.

Putting your skills into practice

 **ACTIVITY 5**

Now practise using the skills you have acquired in the previous activities.

Read the poem on the next page carefully and make some notes on the following points:

● What you think the poem is about.

● The ideas the poet may have wanted us to think about.

● The mood and atmosphere created.

● Key words or phrases that stand out to you and the effect they have on you.

● Anything you can say about the way the poem is structured or organised.

● Your response to the poem.

> ! **TIP**
>
> Remember to always back up your point with evidence from the text when you write about the effect of words and phrases.

'Playgrounds', by Berlie Doherty

Playgrounds are such gobby places.
Know what I mean?
Everyone seems to have something to
Talk about, giggle, whisper, scream and shout
about.
I mean, it's like being in a parrot cage.

And playgrounds are such pushy places.
Know what I mean?
Everyone seems to have to
Run about, jump, kick, do cartwheels,
handstands, fly around.
I mean, it's like being inside a whirlwind.

And playgrounds are such patchy places.
Know what I mean?
Everyone seems to
Go round in circles, lines and triangles,
coloured shapes.
I mean, it's like being in a kaleidoscope.

And playgrounds are such pally places.
Know what I mean?
Everyone seems to
Have best friends, secrets, link arms, be in
gangs.
Everyone except me.

Know what I mean?

127

How to annotate poems

▶ To practise annotating unseen poems.
▶ To make use of annotations when writing a response to unseen poems.

As you already know, making brief notes or annotations around a poem can really help to focus and organise your ideas and zoom in on key words and phrases.

 ACTIVITY 1

Here is an example of a poem that has been partly annotated by a student in preparation for a written response. Look at the annotations and think how you would annotate the rest of the poem. Write down the notes you would make as if you were annotating the poem.

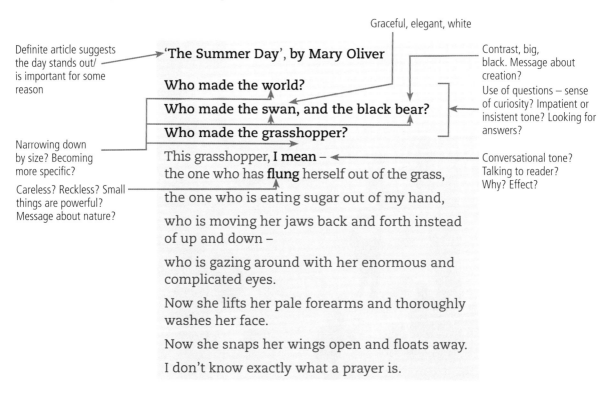

Graceful, elegant, white

Definite article suggests the day stands out/ is important for some reason

Narrowing down by size? Becoming more specific?

Careless? Reckless? Small things are powerful? Message about nature?

Contrast, big, black. Message about creation?

Use of questions – sense of curiosity? Impatient or insistent tone? Looking for answers?

Conversational tone? Talking to reader? Why? Effect?

'The Summer Day', by Mary Oliver

Who made the world?

Who made the swan, and the black bear?

Who made the grasshopper?

This grasshopper, **I mean** –
the one who has **flung** herself out of the grass,

the one who is eating sugar out of my hand,

who is moving her jaws back and forth instead of up and down –

who is gazing around with her enormous and complicated eyes.

Now she lifts her pale forearms and thoroughly washes her face.

Now she snaps her wings open and floats away.

I don't know exactly what a prayer is.

I do know how to pay attention, how to fall
down

into the grass, how to kneel down in the grass,

how to be idle and blessed, how to stroll
through the fields,

which is what I have been doing all day.

Tell me, what else should I have done?

Doesn't everything die at last, and too soon?

Tell me, what is it you plan to do

With your one wild and precious life?

 ## ACTIVITY 2

Look at this student response to the poem and decide whether the
annotations have been helpful.

> The poem is about making the most of life. I feel that it's also about
> enjoying the wonders of nature and how beautiful nature is. I also
> believe it is about noticing the diversity of life because we are side-tracked
> by unimportant things like money, fame, weight, etc.
>   I feel that the poet wants us to think about many things. First of all,
> I think the poet feels that life is a precious gift and we are not taking
> advantage of it by not living life to the full. I also believe the poet wants us to
> think about how amazing life is, but also how short it is and how we forget
> moral values. I also believe that because there is a detailed description of
> nature, the poet wants us to get back to basics and forget technology, enjoy
> plants and nature and the wonderful gift of life.
>   The mood at the start of the poem is hard to work out. The questions
> make it seem like there is a confused mood to the poem. As the poet
> describes the grasshopper, I feel there is a tranquil mood to the poem and there
> is no indication of a negative atmosphere. The mood and atmosphere do change

with the words, 'doesn't everything die at last?' This changes the mood completely and makes the poem a lot more pessimistic. The talk of death gives the poem a gloomy atmosphere and makes the mood a lot more negative and dull.

There are a few words and phrases I find interesting, the first being 'Who made the world?' I find this interesting because it is a rhetorical question and makes the reader feel part of the poem, but also I find it interesting because it is a very philosophical question to begin a poem with. I also find the close description of the grasshopper interesting simply because describing such a small creature is very interesting and unique. The last line, 'with your one wild and precious life?', interests me because it's a rhetorical question and it gives the reader something to think about when the poem has finished.

I really enjoyed the poem. It opened my eyes and made me realise how beautiful everything is and how detailed even the smallest and seemingly unimportant things are. It's extremely engaging and gets you thinking a lot about how amazing life is.

1. Do you think the student has made the best use of the annotations? Explain why or why not.
2. Write down two things you think this answer does well.
3. Write down two things you think the student needs to do to improve the response.

ACTIVITY 3

Look at the Assessment Objectives and marking criteria on pp. 113–17.

Which band do you think this response would fall into, and why?

 ## ACTIVITY 4

If you thought this would be a Band 4 response, you are right! This is a very engaged personal response. The student has a clear understanding of the poet's intentions and has used evidence to support these ideas. However, in order to reach Band 5, the student needs to focus on individual words and phrases, and to consider the effects they have on the reader. For example, although noted in the annotations, there was no mention of the title. The final question is important to the poem as a whole, and this could have been commented on. The effect of the first person narrator could have been developed. Write a few sentences that could improve the response.

 ## ACTIVITY 5

Now look at this response to the same question and decide how it compares to the first response. Which band do you think this response would come into? Give evidence for your answer.

> The poem begins with questions, 'Who made the world? Who made the swan and the black bear?' These questions give a childish mood to the poem as the language is simple and the fact that the poet goes on to ask more questions without waiting for an answer makes them seem inquisitive and curious. The use of the word 'flung' when the poet describes the grasshopper is unexpected and unusual. Lines 5 and 6 begin with 'who is' and lines 7 and 8 also begin with the same words, 'now she'. These lines describe what the grasshopper is doing and the poet uses very human descriptions, such as 'gazing around', 'lifts her pale forearms' and 'thoroughly washes her face'. The fact that the grasshopper is described as 'she' instead of 'it' adds to the

personalised, human impression. The poem changes abruptly after the grasshopper 'floats away' as the poet says, 'I don't know exactly what a prayer is' and this goes back to the philosophical questions at the beginning of the poem. The poet then contrasts this with, 'I do know how to...' and lists some of the things she knows how to do, interspersing physical things like 'fall down into the grass' with more mental things such as 'pay attention' and 'be idle and blessed'. The poet gives more meaning to the list when she says, 'which is what I have been doing all day'. Then there are more questions, like 'tell me, what else should I have done?' This question sounds almost defensive as if she is asking someone who thinks she should have done something more meaningful. The poet then asks, 'doesn't everything die at last and too soon?' The contrast between 'at last' and 'too soon' creates interest as 'at last' suggests that something dies after a long time, while 'too soon' implies that death comes too early. Here the poet could be suggesting that she might as well 'be idle and blessed' because death could come at any minute and 'at last and too soon' could describe the unexpectedness of death. The poet ends the poem asking what it is 'you plan to do with your one wild and precious life?' Here it seems that the poet is saying that life should be enjoyed because there is 'one' only and it is 'wild and precious'. The poem seems to be exploring philosophical ideas like 'who made the world' and religious ideas like prayer, while references to nature — 'swan', 'black bear', 'grasshopper', 'grass' and 'fields' — lighten the poem whilst adding to the questions, as the grasshopper has 'enormous and complicated eyes' and is 'moving her jaws back and forth instead of up and down'. The poet is musing on the wonders of nature and the world whilst enjoying life and trying to value it.

You will probably have noticed that this response selects key words and phrases and analyses them in considerable detail. Find examples of where the student has done this.

Practising your skills

Now that you have practised annotating a poem and looked at some sample answers, it is time to use these skills!

ACTIVITY 1

Read the poem 'Winter Swans' and write down the brief notes you would make as if you were annotating the poem.

'Winter Swans', by Owen Sheers

The clouds had given their all –
two days of rain and then a break
in which we walked,

the waterlogged earth
gulping for breath at our feet
as we skirted the lake, silent and apart,

until the swans came and stopped us
with a show of tipping in unison.
as if rolling weights down their bodies to their heads

they halved themselves in the dark water,
icebergs of white feather, paused before returning again
like boats righting in rough weather.

'They mate for life' you said as they left,
porcelein over the stilling water. I didn't reply
but as we moved on through the afternoon light,

slow stepping in the lake's shingle and sand,
I noticed our hands, that had, somehow,
swum the distance between us

and folded, one after the other,
like a pair of wings settling after flight.

133

ACTIVITY 2

Now, using your notes to help you, write about the poem and its effect on you.

 ACTIVITY 3

Look back over your response and label it to show where you have written:

- A summary of what the poem is about.
- An understanding of the main ideas or themes of the poem.
- About the significance of the title.
- About the mood and atmosphere created; did you write about the effect of specific words? Did you think the mood and atmosphere remained the same throughout the poem?
- About key words and phrases from each stanza; did you write about the effect of the words you selected?
- About the way the poem is organised or structured.
- Your own personal response to the poem and its ideas.

Which sections of your answer lack details from the poem? Would adding another sentence or two to each paragraph improve your response?

Further practice!

By now you should be feeling a bit more confident about dealing with unseen poems and annotating them in an exam situation.

Look at this next poem, on the following page. In the poem 'Zero Hour', the poet writes about society in the future.

Zero Hour, by Matthew Sweeney

Tomorrow all the trains will stop
and we will be stranded. Cars
have already been immobilised
by the petrol wars, and sit
abandoned, along the roadsides.
The airports, for two days now,
are closed-off zones where dogs
congregate loudly on the runways.
To be in possession of a bicycle
is to risk your life. My neighbour,
a doctor, has somehow acquired a horse
and rides to his practice, a rifle
clearly visible beneath the reins,
I sit in front of the television
for each successive news bulletin
then reach for the whisky bottle.

How long before the shelves are empty
in the supermarkets? The first riots
are raging as I write, and who
out there could have predicted
this sudden countdown to zero hour,
all the paraphernalia of our comfort
stamped obsolete, our memories
fighting to keep us sane and upright?

ACTIVITY 1

Read the poem two or three times, and write down any notes as if you were annotating it. Try to cover the following points:

- A brief overview or summary of what you think the poem is about.
- The main ideas or themes the poet may want you to think about.
- The significance of the title.
- The mood or atmosphere and the words that create this effect.
- Key words, phrases and images and what they make you think of.
- Your response to the poem.

 ACTIVITY 2

Now that you have had a chance to organise your thoughts and ideas about the poem, try writing a response to this exam-style question on the poem.

> Write about the poem 'Zero Hour' by Matthew Sweeney and its effect on you.
> You may wish to consider:
>
> - what the poem is about and how it is organised
> - the ideas the poet may have wanted us to think about
> - the poet's choice of words, phrases and images and the effects they create
> - how you respond to the poem.

 ACTIVITY 3

When you have finished, check that you have:

- written about the main ideas
- selected key words and phrases and explained the effects they create
- given a thoughtful and well-considered personal response.

Moving up the bands

Here are some answers written by students in response to the same question.

 ACTIVITY 1

Read the answers and the comments an examiner has made about them.

Student A

The poem 'Zero Hour' is about war. The poet would have wanted us to see what it was like and how he was feeling. In the poem he sounds scared, sitting and wondering what is going to happen next. This poem is interesting because it's almost as if he's listing and questioning himself about what could or has gone wrong. The phrase I'm most interested in is 'The first riots are raging as I write and who out there could have predicted this sudden countdown to zero hour?' I like this phrase because it relates to the title of the poem. Every poem should have a phrase like that. I think that the poem is lacking rhythm and rhyming words. Poems should be like a little song in your head, but with this poem it didn't really have a rhythm. It felt as if I was just saying it to myself.

Examiner comment: *There is a simple but limited focus on the task. There is a basic understanding of some key aspects of the poem, such as it 'is about war', however the points are never developed or explored. Basic reference is made to meanings and effects ('the poem is lacking rhythm and rhyming words') but examples are not provided. Some comments are simply too vague: 'I like this phrase because it relates to the title of the poem'. The answer is also too brief. The quality of this response would place it in Band 1.*

Student B

The poem is about a 'countdown to zero hour'. The poet wants us to think about life if we thought the world was going to end, or if there was some sort of riot happening. The atmosphere of the poem is very tense and cynical as it isn't a very happy poem, but it is talking about a countdown to the end. I find the phrase 'sit abandoned' interesting when describing the car because I like the way the poet has used a metaphor to create an image of the unused car. I also like the title 'Zero Hour' because I think it's a good way of talking about the end. The rhetorical question is interesting because it makes you think about the poem and I like the way he said the memories are 'fighting' because it shows that it is a big struggle to keep yourself from going insane. I think the poet wanted us to see that the person he is writing about doesn't feel that he has much to live for because all he does is wait for 'successive news' and drink whisky. This shows he has no hope and doesn't think that anything is going to get better. Describing the riots as 'raging' shows that they were really bad, and I think the poet wanted to show this. The fact that his next door neighbour carries a rifle and makes it visible, makes you think about what is actually going on that must be so bad that you are protected and armed every time you leave the house. I like the way that the last lines leave you thinking because of the two rhetorical questions. I think this is what the poet wanted to do and he has succeeded. He wants us to think that having a bicycle is a risk to your life and that 'somehow' his neighbour got a horse, making us wonder what has happened to society.

Examiner comment: *This is an engaged discussion with a personal response to the content of the poem. Ideas are conveyed with general coherence and there is understanding of the key points of the poem. The student supports and justifies comments through referring to the text and by using quotations. Some meanings are discussed, such as the reference to the memories and the hopelessness of the character. However, there could have been greater focus on key words and phrases, together with more detailed explanation of their effects. The quality of this response would place it in Band 3.*

Student C

This poem is a description of either the country or world descending into chaos. The title 'Zero Hour' suggests the end of time or the end of the world. The final stanza mentions the 'sudden countdown to zero hour' suggesting this poem describes the last few days or weeks before the world as we know it, ends. The poet may have wanted us to think about how much we take for granted and question what really matters, and how long it will last. We do not know how long the world will be as we know it so we shouldn't just assume things will stay as they are and should think about the consequences of our actions.

This poem has a very negative mood. Words such as 'stranded', 'immobilised' and 'abandoned' add to this. There is also an element of danger since the poet writes that something as basic as owning a bike is 'to risk your life'. There is a feeling of panic and urgency brought about by words such as 'countdown' and rhetorical questions beginning with 'how long...'.

The poem seems very organised with each stanza having the same number of lines. However, the way the lines are written, with pauses sometimes in the middle and sometimes at the end, makes it seem like there is chaos within the structure, perhaps relating to the poem's content.

The poem doesn't rhyme, making it seem more like a story or a description than a poem. This adds to the seriousness of the content. The poem is organised into three stanzas; the first describing the situation on a national or global level; the second on a smaller scale, the man's area; and the third is about how the situation affects his personality.

The ambiguity as to the cause of the situation in stanza one draws the reader in, making them interested in what is happening. The line 'all the paraphernalia of our comfort stamped obsolete' suggests to the reader that if the world is ending, personal objects and material goods won't matter.

Animal imagery is used in the first and second stanza with the dogs and horse. The fact that they are mentioned twice adds emphasis suggesting that perhaps without planes and cars, we are like animals.

> *The poem makes me realise what I take for granted. The entire final stanza consists of two rhetorical questions, one asking who could predict when this sort of situation could strike. The answer for me is 'no one' and this shows no matter how big, the world is still fragile.*

Examiner comment: *This response has a clear overview and a real engagement with the content. A sensitive and evaluative approach has been adopted and pertinent, direct references are made across the poem. There is assured reference to meanings and effects are explored. Clear awareness of alternative interpretation is shown through the frequent use of tentative language. The quality of this response would place it in Band 5.*

 ACTIVITY 2

(1) Look at your own response to this question. How do you think it compares to these three answers? Which band do you think your answer was closest to?

(2) What do you think you need to do to improve your answer? Write down three things you will aim to improve upon next time.

Comparing two poems

▶ To develop the skills required to compare two poems.
▶ To practise writing a comparison between two poems.

Now that you feel more confident about dealing with unseen poems and annotating them, it is time to turn your attention to focus on the type of question you will face in Section C part (b).

This is the part of the exam where you will be expected to write about and compare two unseen poems. The two poems will have been chosen because there will be some sort of link between them, and the question will draw your attention to this link. The poems will usually be connected by their content or theme. For example, both poems might be about the theme of growing up, or the theme of nature. Sometimes you might notice that the structure of both poems is very similar or different. Perhaps one poem is written in the first person while the other is written in the third person, and this could be a useful point to consider in your response.

 ACTIVITY 1

In the first section of this book, you have already come across words that would draw the examiner's attention to the fact that you are comparing and/or contrasting aspects of the poems.

Quickly list as many of these words as you can remember under these headings.

Words to show similarities	Words to show differences
likewise	unlike

ACTIVITY 2

Read the two poems that follow. In the first poem, the poet writes from the point of view of a city; in the second, the poet writes from the point of view of a river.

'Song of the City', by Gareth Owen

My brain is stiff with concrete
My limbs are rods of steel
My belly's stuffed with money
My soul was bought in a deal.

They poured metal through my arteries
They choked my lungs with lead
They churned my blood to plastic
They put murder in my head.

I'd a face like a map of the weather
Flesh that grew to the bone
But they tore my story out of my eyes
And turned my heart to stone.

Let me wind from my source like a river
Let me grow like wheat from the grain
Let me hold out my arms like a natural tree
Let my children love me again.

'The River's Story', by Brian Patten

I remember when life was good.
I shilly-shallied across meadows,
Tumbled down mountains,
I laughed and gurgled through woods,
Stretched and yawned in a myriad of floods.
Insects, weightless as sunbeams,
Settled on my skin to drink.
I wore lily-pads like medals.
Fish, lazy and battle scarred,
Gossiped beneath them.
The damselflies were my ballerinas,
The pike my ambassadors.
Kingfishers, disguised as rainbows,
Were my secret agents.

It was a sweet time, a gone-time,
A time before factories grew,
Brick by greedy brick,
And left me cowering in monstrous shadows.
Like drunken giants
They vomited their poisons into me.
Tonight a scattering of vagrant bluebells,
Dwarfed by those same poisons,
Toll my ending.

Children, come and find me if you wish,
I am your inheritance.
Behind the derelict housing estates
You will discover my remnants.
Clogged with garbage and junk
To an open sewer I've shrunk.
I, who have flowed through history,
Have seen hamlets become villages,
Villages become towns, towns become cities,
Am reduced to a trickle of filth
Beneath the still, burning stars.

ACTIVITY 3

Work through the following points to help develop and consolidate your understanding of both poems.

Let's start by considering 'Song of the City' in more detail. Read the poem through carefully two or three times, remembering the advice you were given in the previous section about how to 'read' a poem. You might find it helpful to make some notes about the following points:

- What do you think is happening in each stanza? (content)
- What do you think the theme or the main idea of the poem might be? What do you think the writer is trying to tell us?
- Do you think the title is significant in any way?
- What is the mood and atmosphere of the poem? How does the poet create this mood or atmosphere? Do you think there is a change in the mood and atmosphere during the course of the poem? If so, where and how has the poet shown this change?
- Select and make notes on the words, phrases and images you find interesting or effective.
- How is the poem structured and organised? What effect does this have?
- How do you respond to the poem, as a whole?

 TIP

Remember that the first and most important thing is to understand what the poems are about before you consider how they are similar and/or different. You will be given credit for discussing the content and ideas in the poems, supported by reference to the text.

 ACTIVITY 4

Now you should consider 'The River's Story' in more detail. Read the poem through carefully two or three times, remembering the advice you were given in the previous section about how to 'read' a poem. You might find it helpful to make some notes about the points listed in Activity 3 above.

ACTIVITY 5

Now that you have worked through both poems, you can start to think about the ways in which they are similar and/or different. Look at the table below. Copy it and write down your ideas under the separate headings.

	'Song of the City'	'The River's Story'
Subject matter (content)		
Main ideas/message (theme)		
The title		
Mood and atmosphere		
Words, phrases and images		
Structure and organisation		
Your individual response		

 ACTIVITY 6

Now that you have had time to organise your thoughts about the poem, try writing a response to the following exam-style question of the type you would see in Section C part (b).

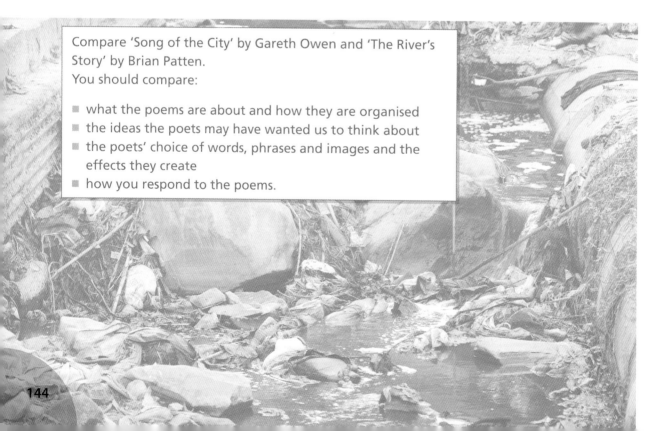

Compare 'Song of the City' by Gareth Owen and 'The River's Story' by Brian Patten.
You should compare:

- what the poems are about and how they are organised
- the ideas the poets may have wanted us to think about
- the poets' choice of words, phrases and images and the effects they create
- how you respond to the poems.

ACTIVITY 7

When you have finished, look back over your answer and annotate it to show where you have included the following:

- Discussion of what both poems are about.
- Discussion of the main ideas or themes in the poems.
- Discussion of the words, phrases and images in the poems.
- Specific details, evidence or quotes from the poems to support your points.
- Discussion of similarities and/or differences between the poems.
- A well-considered personal response.

 ACTIVITY 8

1. What do you think you need to do in order to improve your response?
2. Have a look at the marking criteria on pp. 116–117 and decide on three things you could do to improve your performance.
3. Keeping these improvements in mind, write down two targets for the next time you compare unseen poems.

Developing skills and confidence

The following activity will give you further practice and develop your confidence when tackling and comparing unseen poems.

 ACTIVITY 1

Look at the following poems, 'Rejection' by Jenny Sullivan and 'Years Ago' by Elizabeth Jennings.

 TIP

In the exam, you are advised to spend approximately one hour on Section C. This would probably suggest that you need to spend approximately 20 minutes writing about the single unseen poem in part (a) because it is worth 15 marks and approximately 40 minutes writing about the second unseen poem and comparing in part (b) because it is worth 25 marks.

In both poems people reflect on relationships that have gone wrong.

'Rejection', by Jenny Sullivan

Rejection is orange
Not, as one might think,
Grey and nondescript.
It is the vivid orange of
A council worker's jacket.
A coat of shame that says
'he doesn't want you.'

Rejection tastes like ashes
Acrid, bitter.
It sounds
Like the whisper of voices
Behind my back.
'he didn't want her.
He dumped her.'
It feels
Like the scraping of fingernails
On a blackboard,
Not ache or stab of pain
But like having
A layer of skin missing.
Rejection looks like – me,
I suppose.

Slightly leftover
Like the last, curled sandwich
When all the guests
Have gone.

'Years Ago', by Elizabeth Jennings

It was what we did not do that I
remember,
Places with no markers left by us,
All of a summer, meeting every day,
A memorable summer of hot days,
Day after day of them, evening after
evening.
Sometimes we would laze

Upon the river-bank, just touching hands
Or stroking one another's arms with
grasses.
Swans floated by seeming to assert
Their dignity. But we too had our own
Decorum* in the small-change of first love.

Nothing was elegiac* or nostalgic,
We threw time in the river as we threw
Breadcrumbs to an inquisitive duck, and
so
Day entered evening with a sweeping
gesture,
Idly we talked of food and where to go.

This is the love that I knew long ago.
Before possession, passion, and betrayal.

Decorum – suitable behaviour
Elegiac – mournful or sad

ACTIVITY 2

First of all consider 'Rejection' in more detail to consolidate your understanding.

Read the poem through carefully two or three times. You might find it helpful to make some notes about the following points:

- What do you think is happening in each stanza? (content) Do you understand what the poem is about?
- What do you think the theme or the main idea of the poem might be? What do you think the writer is trying to tell us?
- Do you think the title is significant in any way?
- Who do you think is speaking the poem? Do you think this could be important in any way?
- What is the mood and atmosphere of the poem? How does the poet create this mood or atmosphere?
- Select and make notes on the words, phrases and images you find interesting or effective.
- How is the poem structured and organised? What effect does this have?
- How do you respond to the poem, as a whole?

 ACTIVITY 3

Now look at 'Years Ago' in more detail and consider the following points to help you to organise your thoughts and ideas:

- What do you think is happening in each stanza? (content) Do you understanding what the poem is about?
- What do you think the theme or the main idea of the poem might be? What do you think the writer is trying to tell us?
- Do you think the title is significant in any way?
- Who do you think is 'speaking' the poem? Do you think this could be important in any way?
- What is the mood and atmosphere of the poem? How does the poet create this mood or atmosphere? Do you think there is a change in the mood and atmosphere during the course of the poem? If so, where and how has the poet shown this change?
- Select and make notes on the words, phrases and images you find interesting or effective.
- How is the poem structured and organised? What effect does this have?
- How do you respond to the poem, as a whole?

ACTIVITY 4

Now that you have had an opportunity to gather your thoughts about both poems, you need to consider how they are similar and/or different.

Look at the table below. Copy it and write down your ideas under the separate headings.

	'Rejection'	'Years Ago'
Subject matter (content)		
Main ideas/message (theme)		
The title		
Mood and atmosphere		
Words, phrases and images		
Structure and organisation		
Your individual response		

Or you might prefer to use the following type of diagram to help you shape and collate your ideas about the similarities and differences between the two poems.

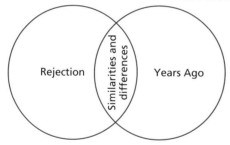

 ACTIVITY 5

Now using the targets you set yourself on page 145 and the information from your answers to the previous activities, write your response to the following exam-style question:

Compare 'Rejection' by Jenny Sullivan and 'Years Ago' by Elizabeth Jennings.
You should compare:

- what the poems are about and how they are organised
- the ideas the poets may have wanted us to think about
- the poets' choice of words, phrases and images and the effects they create
- how you respond to the poems.

ACTIVITY 6

When you have finished, look back over your answer and annotate it to show where you have included the following:

- Discussion of what both poems are about.
- Discussion of the main ideas or themes in the poems.
- Discussion of the words, phrases and images in the poems.
- Specific details, evidence or quotes from the poems to prove your points.
- Discussion of similarities and/or differences between the poems.
- A well-considered personal response.

 ACTIVITY 7

(1) Read the following student response to the exam-style question you have just tackled and the examiner's comments on that response.

! TIP

It is worth remembering that there is no one 'set' way to answer a question like this. You could write about the second poem (you will have written about the first poem in part (a)) and then write about the similarities and differences between the two poems at the end of your response. Or, you could compare and contrast the poems where appropriate throughout your answer as a whole.

Student A

The poem 'Rejection' is about a woman who is rejected. The evidence showing this is the title and her saying 'Rejection looks like me, I suppose.' Maybe she's the one always getting rejected or the one that rejects others.

The writer of this poem, Jenny Sullivan, has put in different senses. She's written about the feel and the sound. She's also used metaphors, like 'It is the vivid orange/of a council worker's jacket/a coat of shame'. She's also used colours for different moods.

The mood of this poem is upsetting and depressing but the use of adjectives and metaphors is interesting. Like, it says that 'rejection tastes like ashes/acrid, bitter'. The writer has said in the poem 'Behind my back/"He didn't want her./He dumped her."' It's like she can hear that. She relates to herself as 'the last curled sandwich/when all the guests/have gone' which shows that she's been left and that she is lonely and alone.

In the poem 'Years Ago' it seems more happy and calming. It sounds like what could have happened before the story in the poem of 'Rejection'. The poet, Elizabeth Jennings, is talking about her past 'love' and she uses first person language. She's talking about herself and what she remembers from a 'memorable summer'. She mentions there being no 'elegiac'. She says 'we threw time in the river as we threw/breadcrumbs to an inquisitive duck' which tells us that she didn't care about the time she was having with this lover. She's used a good understanding metaphor in this sentence. In the last bit of the poem, she says about that being the love that she knew long ago before 'possession, passion and betrayal'. Maybe she means that's the only memory she has of happiness from being with this person. Maybe he hurt her and then betrayed her. This poem has a happy feeling until the end when the poem has a sad feeling.

The poem 'Years Ago' seems to be telling a story of a past memory, unlike the 'Rejection' poem. 'Rejection' is explaining her feelings and describing them with the taste 'like ashes' and 'the scraping of fingernails'. In terms of each poem's mood 'Years Ago' seems happier than 'Rejection'. 'Years Ago' has some sort of mystery about the 'betrayal, passion and possession' at the end of the poem. Maybe the title is linked to it. Maybe she got her heart broken and now she's decided to write about her past? Both poems are different. They both have different uses of verbs, adverbs and they both have different moods. Also, one poet is talking about herself in the past and the other is talking about herself being rejected and it sounds as if it was during the time she was writing the poem. She sounds like she is feeling sorry for herself.

Examiner comment: *The response shows an understanding of what the poems are about in a straightforward way. Appropriate direct reference to the text is made and the response begins to look at language and form. Some reference is made to meanings but it is not sustained or detailed. There is some discussion of the similarities and/or differences between the poems. The quality of this response would place it at the bottom of Band 3.*

(2) Write down three things you think this student could do to improve this answer.

(3) Select three sentences from the response that you could rewrite, improve and add to, then do this.

ACTIVITY 8

(1) Now read the following student response to the same exam-style question and the examiner's comments on that response. Consider what makes this response more successful than the response in Activity 7.

Student B

In the poem 'Years Ago', Elizabeth Jennings is far more nostalgic about the good times in the relationship, rather than describing her pain like Jenny Sullivan in 'Rejection'. Her relationship took place in 'all of a summer' which suggests that the relationship was good during the time of light and sunshine but possibly suggests that when the winter and the difficult times came, it did not last. The idea of 'hot days' suggests that the summer was filled with the good, warm and caring side of love before the 'possession' that she mentions at the end of the poem, which suggests that the relationship became too intense for her partner.

The use of heat imagery is similar to the fire imagery used in 'Rejection' where the end of the relationship was like 'ashes'. This suggests that the best times during the relationship were like a fire.

Jennings presents a picture of a very happy and calm relationship where they were 'touching hands'. This creates a sense of innocence in their early relationship because they are content with minimal contact rather than having strong sexual desire. This is consolidated by the image that the 'swans floated' which suggests a calm surface to the relationship. The whiteness of the swans implies a sense of purity between the two people. This use of colour imagery is similar to that used by Sullivan in her poem in describing rejection as 'orange'. Both poets use colour to convey a strong sense of how the character feels.

Jennings' poem is slightly ironic as she describes her relationship as being not 'nostalgic' but as she is writing with hindsight her language and the image she portrays of 'swans' and 'decorum' imply that she misses it. She is regretful of the things that they 'did not do', saying that they 'threw time into the river' showing that she wishes she could get back the time which she spent with him to use it better. I could suggest she feels that if she had been more attentive than she was she might not have lost the relationship and therefore she blames herself for the loss. This is quite similar to the way that Sullivan suggests she is the 'last curled sandwich', implying that she is the one that nobody will ever want, and possibly blaming herself for the end of the relationship.

In the same way that Sullivan's 'Rejection' has a different tone at the ending, Jennings' 'Years Ago' becomes far more bitter in the final couplet. It is the only time she expresses truly strong emotion, 'possession, passion and betrayal', which suggests that the surfacing of these emotions was what brought about the end of the relationship. It is quite ambiguous about who felt these emotions, suggesting that it might have been that the author does not want to admit it. 'Betrayal' implies that the other person let her down and stopped loving her, possibly meaning that he had an affair.

Both 'Rejection' and 'Years Ago' are written in the first person, which makes the reader feel involved in the poem. It could be because they want the reader to understand just how personal and painful rejection of love is, or how unpleasant it is to love someone unrequitedly. However, the tone of 'Rejection' is far more bitter and emotional than 'Years Ago'. This is possibly because of the timescale of the poem, as 'Rejection' appears to be far more raw emotionally, talking about feelings immediately after the relationship broke down rather than in 'Years Ago' where it appears to be more nostalgic, sentimental and less bitter until the very end, suggesting that the relationship is older. The author of 'Rejection' appears much more concerned about people talking about her, suggesting she must have been quite young when the relationship ended and therefore feeling rejection for the first time. This is consolidated by the strength of the bitterness in 'Rejection' compared to the softer tone in 'Years Ago'.

> *In conclusion, both poems describe rejection but from different viewpoints. The language in 'Rejection' is far more modern than in 'Years Ago', indicating a younger person. The intense feelings suggests a far more intense relationship than in 'Years Ago'.*

Examiner comment: *This response is sensitive and evaluative, analysing the poems in detail and producing perceptive conclusions. There is evidence of pertinent and direct references across both texts. The appreciation of the poets' use of language is detailed, and meanings and effects are explored in detail. There is a wide-ranging discussion of the similarities and/or differences between the poems. The quality of this response would place it at the top of Band 5.*

2. Select three things from the response that you think the student does very well.

3. Write down examples of where the student has suggested that there could be more than one way of interpreting a word or meaning in the poem.

4. Write down three examples of where the student has analysed the effect of language or images in detail.

ACTIVITY 9

Now that you have considered these sample responses, which one do you think is closest to your own response to the task?

Look at the marking criteria on pp. 116–17 and decide which band you think your response would fall into.

1. Which skills do you think you have improved on since the start of this section?

2. Which skills do you still need to work on and develop in order to improve your performance?

3. How will you make and achieve these improvements?

Approaching the examination – the unseen element

In Component 2 Section C part (a), the single unseen poem, you should be able to write about what the poem is about (content); how it is organised (structure); how the writer creates effects (language, techniques and word choices); your personal response to the poem.

In Component 2 Section C part (b), the unseen poetry comparison, you should be able to write about what the poems are about (content); how they are organised (structure); how the writers create effects (language, techniques and word choices); similarities and/or differences between the poems; your personal response to the poems.

Planning your comparison is vital if you want to score highly. You might want to list the ideas and features you are going to compare and then jot down the details and quotes that you intend to use to support the points you will make.

Preparation is the key to success here! Long before you take the exam, you need to become familiar with the kind of question that you may be asked. You will have already looked at and practised several exam-style questions in this book to help you develop your skills and increase your confidence.

This is how the questions will be structured.

Part (a) will tell you to read the two poems printed on the paper, which will be linked by a particular theme or idea (the question will tell you exactly what the linking theme is to get you started!).

You will then be told to write about the first poem and its effect on you, and the following bullet points will be provided to help structure your ideas:

> You may wish to consider:
> - what the poem is about and how it is organised
> - the ideas the poet may have wanted us to think about
> - the poet's choice of words, phrases and images and the effects they create
> - how you respond to the poem.

> ### ! TIP
>
> Part (a) (the single unseen poem) is worth 15 marks and part (b) (the unseen poetry comparison) is worth 25 marks, so this would suggest that you need to spend more time answering part (b).
>
> You are advised to spend one hour answering Section C as a whole, therefore you could divide your time by spending approximately 20 minutes on part (a) and 40 minutes on part (b).

Part (b) will tell you to compare the second poem with the first poem, and the following bullet points will be provided to help structure your ideas.

> You should compare:
> - what the poems are about and how they are organised
> - the ideas the poets may have wanted us to think about
> - the poets' choice of words, phrases and images and the effects they create
> - how you respond to the poems.

You should remember to use vocabulary to signal to the examiner where you are writing about similarities and/or differences.

How can I do well in Component 2 Section C?

The examination is your opportunity to put into practice and show off all the skills you have been learning in these activities. Now your next challenge is to work out how to organise and structure your response to score the highest marks you can. You might find it helpful to follow this plan of action.

Read the question and the poems very carefully. Underline or highlight the key words in the poems and decide what effects are being created. Remember to keep the Assessment Objectives (AO1 and AO2) in mind because you will need to focus on them in your writing.

Plan carefully and take a few minutes to gather your thoughts and ideas about both poems. Remember that this time is vital in making sure that your comments are organised and that you have enough to write about! In part (b), to achieve a mark in Band 5, you will have to produce a comparison that is 'critical, illuminating and sustained across Assessment Objectives AO1 and AO2'. This suggests it would be sensible to draw up a quick list of similarities and differences before you start writing.
However, it does not mean that every point you make has to be compared! Jot down some of the key ideas and themes from both poems and a few of the details you might want to explore and analyse. Do not panic about your timing. This is time well spent, and five minutes planning time here will ensure your writing is coherent, focused and detailed.

Write with confidence! You should aim to write about the content, themes, language, structure and your response to the poems. This might sound daunting but remember to be **selective**! You will not be able or be expected to cover every detail about the poems in the time allowed – write about the poems in the ways you have practised in this section.

Check your work if you have any time left at the end of the examination, and decide whether you could improve your answer in any way. For example, could you add another sentence to explain the effect of a

particular word or image? Could you make another point about the
similarities and/or differences between the poems? Could you include an
extra sentence to describe your reaction to the poem? Making
improvements like this might score you an extra mark or two! Do not worry
about checking errors in spelling or punctuation because they do not carry
any marks in this section.

Now it's time to **practise planning an exam response**.

Here is an exam-style question:

> Read the poems 'Tramp' by Rupert M. Loydell and
> 'Decomposition' by Zulfikar Ghose.
>
> **Both of these poems describe people's reactions to
> individuals on the edge of society.**

'Tramp' by Rupert M. Loydell

This mad prophet
gibbers mid-traffic
wringing his hands
whilst mouthing at heaven.

No messages for us.
His conversation is simply
a passage through time.
He points and calls

Our uneven stares dissuade
approach. We fear him, his
matted hair, patched coat,
grey look from sleeping out.

We mutter amongst ourselves
and hope he keeps away. No
place for him in our heaven,
there it's clean and empty.

'Decomposition' by Zulfikar Ghose

I have a picture I took in Bombay
of a beggar asleep on the pavement:
grey-haired, wearing shorts and a dirty shirt,
his shadow thrown aside like a blanket.

His arms and legs could be cracks in the stone;
routes for the ants' journeys, the flies' descents.

Brain-washed by the sun into exhaustion.
he lies veined into stone, a fossil man.

Behind him, there is a crowd passingly
bemused by a pavement trickster and quite
indifferent to this very common sight
of an old man asleep on the pavement.

I thought it was a good composition
and glibly called it The Man in the Street,
remarking how typical it was of
India that the man in the street lived there.

His head in the posture of one weeping
into a pillow chides me now for my
presumption at attempting to compose
art out of his hunger and solitude.

a) Write about the poem 'Tramp' by Rupert M. Loydell and its effect on you. (15)

You may wish to consider:

- what the poem is about and how it is organised
- the ideas the poet may have wanted us to think about
- the poet's choice of words, phrases and images and the effects they create
- how you respond to the poem.

b) Now compare 'Tramp' by Rupert M. Loydell and 'Decomposition' by Zulfikar Ghose. (25)

You should compare:

- what the poems are about and how they are organised
- the ideas the poets may have wanted us to think about
- the poets' choice of words, phrases and images and the effects they create
- how you respond to the poems.

Write a quick plan in response to this question. You could use a diagram like the one below to help you.

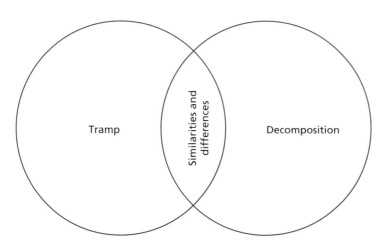

Improving a sample response

Read this extract discussing the similarities and/or differences between the poems from a sample student response:

> The mood of 'Tramp' is quite pessimistic. It shows the hatred towards the homeless and shows the negative impact it might have on others, 'no place for him in our heaven, there it's clean and empty'. The mood in the last stanza is thought-provoking, making you think why people are so judgemental towards them. Similarly in 'Decomposition' the mood is again pessimistic, 'a dirty shirt'. This shows that the beggar is not well presented, being 'dirty' and this isn't pleasant. This poem is also thought-provoking. 'He lies veined into stone, a fossil man.' This quote makes the atmosphere of the poem interesting by using imagery.

Look at the Assessment Objectives and marking criteria on pp. 113–17 and try to decide which band this response would fall into. Work out what you think the student would need to do to improve this response.

Now look at this next response to the same question and work out why it is better than the first one.

> These two poems are very similar and are equally powerful in describing society's outcasts. They both describe homeless men who have no choice but to live on the streets. Both wear dirty clothes and are described using the bland, bleak colour 'grey'. Neither man is recognised, although in 'Tramp' he does his best to get noticed by the public, although they 'dissuade' his approach. Although these two poems have the same main theme, there are subtle differences – one man screams and 'gibbers mid-traffic' for attention, while in 'Decomposition' the man simply lies on the floor – 'his head in the posture of one weeping into a pillow'. The man in 'Tramp' is feared as he is possibly mad, while the tramp in 'Decomposition' is noticed by only one person, the poet. The rest are 'bemused by a pavement trickster'.

Paired poems

as
like
smile
almost
good
I
it
sacred
look
home
wild
on
of
dazzle
embrace
life
no
or
ghost
than
on
poetry

OBJECTIVE

▶ To develop and practise writing about and comparing unseen poems.

Now that you know how to read, annotate and make comparisons between unseen poems, the only way to develop these skills and improve your confidence is to practise, practise and practise!

In this section you will have five 'sets' of paired unseen poems to work on, with some questions to get you started and exam-style questions for you to answer.

Pair A

Look at the following poems, 'Strongman' by Tony Curtis and 'On Ageing' by Maya Angelou.

In both poems people reflect on old age.

'Strongman', by Tony Curtis

A strongman, you say,
Home from work, would stretch his arms
And hang his five sons from them,
Turning like a roundabout.
A carpenter, he could punch nails
Into wood with a clenched fist,
Chest like a barrel with a neck
That was like holding on to a tree.

In the final hour
Your hands between the sheets
To lift him to the lavatory
Slipped under a frame of bones like plywood.
'No trouble,' he said. 'No trouble, Dad,'
You said. And he died in the cradle of your arms.

'On Ageing', by Maya Angelou

When you see me sitting quietly,
Like a sack left on the shelf,
Don't think I need your chattering,
I'm listening to myself.
Hold! Stop! Don't pity me!
Hold! Stop your sympathy!
Understanding if you get it,
Otherwise I'll do without it!

When my bones are stiff and aching
And my feet won't climb the stairs,
I will only ask one favour:
Don't bring me no rocking chair.
When you see me walking, stumbling,
Don't study and get it wrong.
'Cause tired don't mean lazy
And every goodbye ain't gone.
I'm the same person I was back then,
A little less hair, a little less chin,
A lot less lungs and much less wind,
But ain't I lucky I can still breathe in.

 ACTIVITY 1

Now answer this exam-style question:

> Compare 'Strongman' by Tony Curtis and 'On Ageing' by Maya Angelou.
>
> You should compare:
>
> - what the poems are about and how they are organised
> - the ideas the poets may have wanted us to think about
> - the poets' choice of words, phrases and images and the effects they create
> - how you respond to the poems.

Can't think how to start your sentences? Here are some useful sentence starters to help you write about similarities and/or differences:

Similarities	Differences
The poems both have…	Whereas in …, in…
Both poets decided to…	While … has …, in… there is…
In both poems…	However, in … we see a different…
There are obvious similarities in the poets' use of…	It is very different in … however, as we notice that…
We can see some obvious links/similarities in the…	On the other hand, … has…
Neither of the poets chose to…	Another important difference can be seen as…
In neither of the poems is there any…	
There is an important link/similarity between the poems as…	
Another link between the poems is…	

 ACTIVITY 2

Look back at your answer and annotate it to show where you have:

- provided a detailed discussion of both poems
- supported your points with evidence or quotations from the poems
- focused on words, phrases and images and discussed their effectiveness in detail
- discussed the mood and atmosphere of both poems
- written about the similarities and/or differences between the poems
- given a thoughtful and sensitive personal response to the poems.

 ACTIVITY 3

Look at the marking criteria on pp. 116–117 and decide which band you think your response would fall into.

What do you think you need to do to improve your performance next time?

Pair B

Look at the following poems, 'First Ice' by Andrei Voznesensky and 'Manwatching' by Georgia Garrett.

Both poems are about relationships and the pain that love can cause.

'First Ice', by Andrei Voznesensky

A girl freezes in a telephone booth.
In her draughty overcoat she hides
A face all smeared
In tears and lipstick.
She breathes on her thin palms.
Her fingers are icy. She wears earrings.

She'll have to go home alone, alone
Along the icy street.

First ice. It is the first time.
The first ice of telephone phrases.

Frozen tears glitter on her cheeks.
The first ice of human hurt.

'Manwatching', by Georgia Garrett

From across the party I watch you
Watching her.
Do my possessive eyes
Imagine your silent messages?
I think not.
She looks across at you
And telegraphs her flirtatious reply.
I have come to recognise this code.
You are on intimate terms with this pretty stranger,
And there is nothing I can do.
My face is calm, expressionless
But my eyes burn into your back
While my insides shout with rage.
She weaves her way towards you
Turning on a bewitching smile.
I can't see your face, but you are mesmerised,
I expect.
I can predict you: I know this scene so well.
Some acquaintance grabs your arm,
You turn and meet my accusing stare head on.
Her eyes follow yours, meet mine
And then slide away, she understands.
She's not interested enough to compete.
It's over now.
She fades away, you drift towards me.
'I'm bored' you say, without a trace of guilt.
So we go.
Passing the girl in the hall.
'Bye' I say frostily.
I suppose
You winked.

ACTIVITY 1

Now answer this exam-style question:

> Compare 'First Ice' by Andrei Voznesensky and 'Manwatching'
> by Georgia Garrett.
> You should compare:
>
> ■ what the poems are about and how they are organised
> ■ the ideas the poets may have wanted us to think about
> ■ the poets' choice of words, phrases and images and the
>   effects they create
> ■ how you respond to the poems.

Here are a few sentence starters for when you want to focus on individual words or lines:

- This word suggests that...
- This phrase implies that...
- The poet's use of the word '...' tells us that...
- When we read this line/word, we feel... because...
- The poet deliberately uses this word to make us feel...
- In the next line we see that there is...
- This line is important because...
- This word is particularly striking as we feel...
- This word is used to emphasise...

ACTIVITY 2

Look back at your answer and annotate it to show where you have:

- provided a detailed discussion of both poems
- supported your points with evidence or quotations from the poems
- focused on words, phrases and images and discussed their effectiveness in detail
- discussed the mood and atmosphere of both poems
- written about the similarities and/or differences between the poems
- given a thoughtful and sensitive personal response to the poems.

 **ACTIVITY 3**

Look at the marking criteria on pp. 116–17 and decide which band you think your response would fall into.

What do you think you need to do to improve your performance next time?

Pair C

Look at the following poems, 'Wind' by Ted Hughes and 'Hurricane' by James Berry.

Both poems are about the power of nature.

'Wind', by Ted Hughes

This house has been far out at sea all night,

The woods crashing through darkness, the booming hills,

Winds stampeding the fields under the window

Floundering black astride and blinding wet

Till day rose; then under an orange sky

The hills had new places, and wind wielded

Blade-light, luminous black and emerald,

Flexing like the lens of a mad eye.

At noon I scaled along the house-side as far as

The coal-house door. Once I looked up –

Through the brunt wind that dented the balls of my eyes

The tent of the hills drummed and strained its guyrope,

The fields quivering, the skyline a grimace,

At any second to bang and vanish with a flap;

The wind flung a magpie away and a black-

Back gull bent like an iron bar slowly. The house

'Hurricane', by James Berry

Under low black clouds

The wind was all

Speedy feet, all horns and breath,

All bangs, howls, rattles,

In every hen house,

Church hall and school.

Roaring, screaming, returning,

It made forced entry, shoved walls,

Made rifts, brought roofs down,

Hitting rooms to sticks apart.

It wrung soft banana trees,

Broke tough trunks of palms.

It pounded vines of yams,

Left fields battered up.

Invisible with such ecstasy –

With no intervention of sun or man –

Everywhere kept changing branches.

Zinc sheets are kites.

Leaves are panic swarms.

Fowls are fixed with feathers turned.

Goats, dogs, pigs

Rang like some fine green goblet in the note

That any second would shatter it. Now deep

In chairs, in front of the great fire, we grip

Our hearts and cannot entertain book,
thought,

Or each other. We watch the fire blazing,

And feel the roots of the house move, but
sit on,

Seeing the window tremble to come in,

Hearing the stones cry out under the horizons.

All are people together.

Then growling it slunk away

From muddy, mossy trail and boats

In hedges: and cows, ratbats, trees,

Fish, all dead in the road.

ACTIVITY 1

Now answer this exam-style question:

> Compare 'Wind' by Ted Hughes and 'Hurricane' by James Berry.
> You should compare:
>
> - what the poems are about and how they are organised
> - the ideas the poets may have wanted us to think about
> - the poets' choice of words, phrases and images and the
>   effects they create
> - how you respond to the poems.

 ACTIVITY 2

Look back at your answer and annotate it to show where you have:

- provided a detailed discussion of both poems
- supported your points with evidence or quotations from the poems
- focused on words, phrases and images and discussed their effectiveness
  in detail
- discussed the mood and atmosphere of both poems
- written about the similarities and/or differences between the poems
- given a thoughtful and sensitive personal response to the poems.

 ACTIVITY 3

Look at the marking criteria on pp. 116–17 and decide which band you
think your response would fall into.

What do you think you need to do to improve your performance next time?

Pair D

Look at the following poems, '3 a.m. Feed' by Steven Blyth and 'Night Feed'
by Eavan Boland. In the first poem, a father remembers when his son was a
baby and he fed him in the middle of the night. In the second poem a
mother describes feeding her baby daughter in the very early morning.

'3 a.m. Feed', by Steven Blyth

Soon we abandoned our 'turns'. I volunteered
Finding that, alone, the world hushed, I
could almost hear
It whispered – 'This is your son.'
In the crook of my arm, a perfect fit,
You were those words given weight.
Your fish mobiles made it seem we sat on
a sea bed,
Your bottle a little oxygen tank,
Your gentle sucking like a tick, tick, tick
Timing how long before we had to go up,
Face currents that tugged us apart – the fuss
Of want-to-hold relatives and worse, the
office
That kept me from your first step, first
clear word.
Those moments were in the presence of
grandparents and mum,
Remembered in detail – 'Ten past one,
Blur on the radio: he went from the armchair
To the coffee table.' Still, for me,
Those feeds have equal clarity,
Last week coming so strongly to mind –
Caught T-shirted in a summer storm,
My forearm felt drops as large and warm
As the one I'd splash there to test the
temperature
That white drop would sometimes dribble
Down to my palm – a pearl.

'Night feed', by Eavan Boland

This is dawn
Believe me
This is your season, little daughter.
The moment daisies open.
The hour mercurial* rainwater
Makes a mirror for sparrows.
It's time we drowned our sorrows.

I tiptoe in.
I lift you up
Wriggling
In your rosy, zipped sleeper.
Yes, this is the hour
For the early bird and me
When finder is keeper.

I crook the bottle.
How you suckle!
This is the best I can be,
Housewife
To this nursery
Where you hold on,
Dear life.

A silt* of milk.
The last suck
And now your eyes are open,
Birth-coloured and offended.
Earth wakes.
You go back to sleep.
The feed is ended.

Worms turn.
Stars go in.
Even the moon is losing face.
Poplars* stilt for dawn.
And we begin
The long fall from grace.
I tuck you in.

mercurial – shining
*silt – the last bit at the bottom of
the bottle*
poplars – tall, straight trees

ACTIVITY 1

Now answer this exam-style question:

> Compare '3 a.m. Feed' by Steven Blyth and 'Night Feed' by Eavan Boland.
>
> You should compare:
>
> ■ what the poems are about and how they are organised
> ■ the ideas the poets may have wanted us to think about
> ■ the poets' choice of words, phrases and images and the effects they create
> ■ how you respond to the poems.

 ACTIVITY 2

Look back at your answer and annotate it to show where you have:

- provided a detailed discussion of both poems
- supported your points with evidence or quotations from the poems
- focused on words, phrases and images and discussed their effectiveness in detail
- discussed the mood and atmosphere of both poems
- written about the similarities and/or differences between the poems
- given a thoughtful and sensitive personal response to the poems.

 ACTIVITY 3

Look at the marking criteria on pp. 116–17 and decide which band you think your response would fall into.

What do you think you need to do to improve your performance next time?

Pair E

Look at the following poems, 'Dawn Revisited' by Rita Dove and 'Carpe Diem' by Stewart Conn.

In both these poems the poets write about making the most of every opportunity in life.

'Dawn Revisited', by Rita Dove

Imagine you wake up
with a second chance: The blue jay*
hawks his pretty wares*
and the oak still stands, spreading
glorious shade. If you don't look back,

the future never happens.
How good to rise in sunlight,
in the prodigal smell of biscuits –
eggs and sausage on the grill.
The whole sky is yours

to write on, blown open
to a blank page. Come on,
shake a leg! You'll never know
who's down there, frying those eggs,
if you don't get up and see.

*blue jay – a type of bird
*hawks his pretty wares – draws
   attention to himself
*Carpe Diem – a Latin expression
   meaning 'seize the day'

'Carpe Diem',* by Stewart Conn

From my study window
   I see you
below in the garden, a hand
   here pruning
or leaning across to snip
   a wayward shoot;

a daub of powder-blue in a
   profusion of green,
then next moment, you are
   no longer there –
only to reappear, this time
   perfectly framed

in dappling sunlight, with
   an armful of ivy
you've trimmed, topped by
   hyacinth blooms,
fragrant survivors of last
   night's frost.

And my heart misses a beat
   at love for you,
knowing a time will come
   when you are
no longer there, nor I here
   to watch you

on a day of such simplicity.
   Meantime let us
make sure we clasp each
   shared moment
in cupped hands, like water
   we dare not spill.

ACTIVITY 1

Now answer this exam-style question:

> Compare 'Dawn Revisited' by Rita Dove and 'Carpe Diem' by Stewart Conn.
>
> You should compare:
>
> - what the poems are about and how they are organised
> - the ideas the poets may have wanted us to think about
> - the poets' choice of words, phrases and images and the effects they create
> - how you respond to the poems.

 ACTIVITY 2

Look back at your answer and annotate it to show where you have:

- provided a detailed discussion of both poems
- supported your points with evidence or quotations from the poems
- focused on words, phrases and images and discussed their effectiveness in detail
- discussed the mood and atmosphere of both poems
- written about the similarities and/or differences between the poems
- given a thoughtful and sensitive personal response to the poems.

 ACTIVITY 3

Look at the marking criteria on pp. 116–17 and decide which band you think your response would fall into.

What do you think you need to do to improve your performance next time?

Glossary of key terms

alliteration	repetition of consonant sounds to create effect; for example, 'on scrolls of silver snowy sentences'.
assonance	repetition of similar vowel sounds to create effect; for example, 'home, alone, alone along the icy street'.
atmosphere	the tone or feeling of a poem.
blank verse	a line of poetry in unrhymed *iambic pentameter*.
caesura	a strong pause in a line of poetry.
cliché	something that used to be interesting but has been overused so much that it has become tired and boring.
connotation	associations suggested by words or images.
couplet	a pair of lines that rhyme at the end.
dramatic monologue	a form of poetry in which a single character addresses the reader.
enjambment	a run-on line of poetry that flows from one line into the next or from the end of one stanza into the beginning of the next stanza.
figurative language	language in which the writer communicates something other than the literal meaning of the words, often through *similes* and *metaphors*.
free verse	poetry without a regular pattern of *meter* or rhyme. It is 'free' because it's not restricted to a particular meter and rhyme scheme.
iambic pentameter	an unrhymed line of poetry with stressed and unstressed syllables.
image	a vivid picture created in the mind by the use of certain words.
imagery	figurative language to create effects.
internal rhyme	the placing of rhyming words within a line of poetry.
irony	a contrast between what is said and what is meant; or between what happens and what is expected to happen.
literal language	taking words in their usual or basic sense.

metaphor	a comparison between two things without using the words 'like' or 'as'; for example, 'the rays of the sun were piercing daggers'.
metaphorical language	taking words outside their usual or basic sense.
meter	a measured pattern of rhythm in poetry.
narrative poem	a type of poem that tells a story.
narrator	the voice or speaker of the poem.
octet	an eight-line stanza usually found in a *sonnet*.
onomatopoeia	the use of words to imitate the sounds they make; for example, buzz, crack, plop.
oxymoron	a combination of opposite words for effect; for example, 'a cruel kindness'.
personification	describing an inanimate object as having human qualities; for example, 'fear gripped my heart'.
quotations	words or phrases taken from the poem.
rhyme	words with similar sounds.
rhythm	the beat or musical quality in a line of poetry.
sestet	a six-line stanza usually found in a *sonnet*.
sibilance	a hissing sound effect created by the repetition of the letter 's'; for example, 'whispers informed strangers I was the eldest.'
simile	a comparison between two things using the words 'like' or 'as'; for example, 'the sun's rays were like piercing daggers'.
sonnet	a 14-line poem written in *iambic pentameter*.
stanza	a verse of poetry.
subject matter	the content or what is happening in the poem.
syllable	a word or part of a word that has one separate sound when you say it.
symbol	something concrete that can represent something more.
syntax	the grammatical order of words in a sentence or line of poetry.
theme	an idea or message the poet wants to communicate to the reader.
tone	the feeling or mood of a poem.